A BOYS AND GIRLS
LIFE OF CHRIST

THE NEGRO CHILDREN'S STORY OF THE GOOD SHEPHERD

Por lil brack sheep don strayed away,
Don los in de win' and de rain,
An' de Shepherd He say, "O hirelin',
Go fin' My sheep again."
But de hirelin' frown, "O Shepherd,
Dat sheep am brack and bad."
But de Shepherd He smile like dat lil brack sheep
Was de onliest lamb He had.

And He said, "O hirelin', hasten
For de win' an' de rain am cold;
An' dat lil brack sheep am lonesome
Out dar so far from de fol'."
De hirelin' frown, "O Shepherd,
Dat sheep am all soiled with de clay."
But de Shepherd He smile like de lil brack sheep
Wuz fair as de break o' day.

An' He said, "O hirelin', hasten.
Lo, here am de ninety-an'-nine,
But dar far off from de sheep-fol'
Is dat lil brack sheep ob Mine."
An' de hirelin' frown, "O Shepherd,
De res' ob de sheep am here."
But de Shepherd He smile like dat lil brack sheep
He hol' de mostest dear.

An' de Shepherd go out in de darkness
Where de night was col' an' bleak,
An' dat lil brack sheep He fin' it
An' lay it against His cheek.
An' de hirelin' frown, "O Shepherd,
Don' bring dat sheep to me."
But de Shepherd He smile as He hol' it close
An'—dat lil brack sheep was—me.

The Bible for School and Home

by J. Paterson Smyth

The Book of Genesis

Moses and the Exodus

Joshua and the Judges

The Prophets and Kings

When the Christ Came:
The Highlands of Galilee

When the Christ Came:
The Road to Jerusalem

St. Matthew

St. Mark

A BOYS AND GIRLS
LIFE OF CHRIST

by

J. Paterson Smyth

YESTERDAY'S CLASSICS

ITHACA, NEW YORK

This edition, first published in 2017 by Yesterday's Classics, an imprint of Yesterday's Classics, LLC, is an unabridged republication of the text originally published by Fleming H. Revell Company in 1929. For the complete listing of the books that are published by Yesterday's Classics, please visit www.yesterdaysclassics. com. Yesterday's Classics is the publishing arm of the Baldwin Online Children's Literature Project which presents the complete text of hundreds of classic books for children at www.mainlesson.com.

ISBN: 978-1-63334-094-7

Yesterday's Classics, LLC
PO Box 339
Ithaca, NY 14851

CONTENTS

CONTENTS

From the Author

BOYS AND GIRLS,—

I am trying to tell you the most wonderful story in the whole world.

But I warn you beforehand that you have got to help me. For I want to write not a simple little story for small children, but a real full Life of Christ for thoughtful boys and girls who are willing to think and use their brains. I have a high opinion of your brains if you will only use them, and I have no intention of writing you a mere childish book. You are fit for better things than that.

I have tried to make the chapters short so as not to tire you. Sometimes I cannot do that without spoiling the story, but any longer chapters are divided into parts so that you can stop anywhere whenever you have read enough.

Now, mind, I am trusting you. I cannot tell the story as I want to without your help.

J. P. S.

The Château, Montreal.
Christmas, 1928.

THE FIRST BOOK

Telling how the Lord Jesus came from Heaven to visit this World, which He had made long ago.

Writing the Gospel story.

I

STORIES OF WONDER AND ROMANCE

ONCE upon a time (it was the year A.D. 1630) a strong, rough-looking young foreigner was working in the great shipbuilding yard in Deptford, England. Every day he worked at his bench, every night he slept in the big dormitory shed. He walked and talked and played games with his English comrades as one of themselves. Then one day, when he had thoroughly learned his business, he went home, and the others forgot him.

But later on there came one day to the shipyard a romantic story of a great prince holding court in a foreign land, and later still of a powerful king whose name was famous in Europe. And they learned that this was that young foreigner who had come to learn shipbuilding to teach his people, that he was really a prince of royal blood in disguise, and now sat on the throne of the proudest kingdom in the world, the Emperor of All the Russias. I don't know if he ever came back to visit them again, but I feel sure that they were proud of that romantic story and that old workers in the shipyard would often in their old age boast that they had worked at the bench side by side with the disguised lord of Russia.

There are several stories like this in history of kings and princes going about amongst the people in romantic adventure disguised as ordinary men. We call them "Stories of Wonder and Romance." But, after all, there is not so much of wonder in them. For these disguised kings and princes when they went home to their palaces were still but ordinary men like ourselves, only living in palaces and wearing grand clothing. Young Peter of Russia, with his robes and palaces, was still just an ordinary man, little better than his old comrades in the shipyard.

Just once in the world's history, only once, 1,900 years ago, there was a real startling "Story of Wonder and Romance," the story of an adventure that has stirred the whole world to its depths. It is the *one central wonder-story of the world.*

In a warm, sunny land beyond the sea, two weeks' journey from England, there was a little country boy playing with his comrades on the village green and afterwards working as a carpenter to support his mother, and afterwards murdered by wicked men because of his brave opposition to their wickedness. And then when they buried Him in a tomb, He rose up from the dead.

And so there came the most startling discovery in all history, that this was really the Lord from Heaven in disguise come down from beyond the stars on a visit to this earth, which He Himself had made long ago! If you want a real story of wonder and romance, you surely have it here. It is almost too wonderful for anyone to believe.

I have been asked to try to tell you that story. I refused at first, for I am so afraid of spoiling it. I don't think anyone could tell it properly. But I will try to tell it as well as I can, trusting you to help me.

In telling of His life I ought, of course, to begin at the beginning. But where is the beginning? If I were writing the life, say, of Prince Peter who worked in the shipyard, I should begin at his birth. That is his beginning. But that is not at all the beginning here. In the life of this village Boy (Jesus of Nazareth, He was called), our thought must go back to the eternal World from which He came, the World where He belongs. You know that beyond this world which we see, beyond the blue sky, beyond the stars and planets, is the Real World, the World of Eternities, the World of God and of the holy angels, the World from which this and all worlds come. We cannot see that World. We cannot map out its continents and shores. No gleam of its golden cities has ever touched our eyes. But we believe that it is above us and around us always.

From that unknown World above the sky, Jesus came for the great adventure. In that great central Heaven He had always lived. From His home there in the far-back eternities He had made this world and all the worlds that you see floating in the skies at night. So you see you could never get back to any beginning of His life even if you went back ages and ages before the Genesis story when "in the beginning God created the heavens and the earth," ages and ages before He appeared on earth as a little baby when "Jesus was born in Bethlehem of Judea in the days of Herod the king." But I have only to tell the story of His visit to earth. And since He began His life on earth as a little baby, we have to begin our story there.

II

THE WORLD FROM
WHICH HE CAME

IT will help you to understand that story better if you think for a little while about that world from which He came. He has told us some lovely things about it. Before He came people down here used to wonder about that unknown world above them and often they were frightened about it. When they heard the thunder rolling in the sky, and the fierce storms smashing the trees, and the wild beasts raging in the forest, they would cry to the powers above not to hurt them. And sometimes when they were not frightened, when the sun shone and the world looked beautiful, they would look out on the glory of the sunset like a golden gate of Heaven and wonder what the great God above was like. Did He ever know when they were in trouble? Did He ever care when their child died? Did He ever think about them at all? They did not know.

So they made images to pray to, ugly wooden idols and big golden images to protect them from dangers that might come from that mysterious world. That was the kind of religion they had, not a happy religion, a religion that kept them rather frightened and uneasy.

Think of the delightful surprise when Jesus came down. "Oh, you are all wrong," He said, "about our World above. Wait till I tell you what it really is like." So as He talked to them day by day, they learned very delightful things about that World that He came from.

He told them that it is a very wonderful and glorious World, a World of wonder and romance and beauty where everyone is happy and nobody does wrong. And especially He told them what they loved best of all to hear, that it is an infinitely kindly, friendly World, that they on that side are all keenly interested in us on this side. The galleries of that World are crowded with friendly faces watching with deep interest our lives on earth, wanting to make us happy, wanting to make us good.

"You are never to be afraid of our World," said Jesus. "You are never to be afraid of God except when you are doing wrong. For God is the kindest, tenderest friend you have. Never think of Him as cruel or unkind. When you think of Him, think of the friend who is so interested in you, who cares for you more than a father cares for his child. Whenever you pray to Him always call Him 'Our Father.' "

One day, for instance, He was talking to some people who had been wicked and were sorry for it and afraid that God would not forgive them. So He told them a story of a boy here on earth, a bad boy who ran away from home and nearly broke his father's heart by his wicked life in a big city far away. When all his money was spent and he was starving, he began to be sorry and to long for his old happy home, but he was afraid to go back to face his angry father. At last he ventured timidly to go back, and there on the road back he got the surprise of his life! Instead of the angry father that he expected, lo and behold! at a turning of the road he saw that dear old father hurrying to meet him with a great joy in his heart at getting back his boy from that wicked life.

And Jesus said, That is just like God when you do wrong and are sorry. That is how God feels. That is how our great World above the sky feels. There is pain in God's heart when any of you do wicked things, but "there is joy in the presence of the angels of God over one sinner that repents of doing wrong."

Another day He was sitting with children around Him and a little boy standing at His knee, and He said to the big people there, Do you know what important people these children are? That in our great World above there are angels watching over these boys and girls down here on earth, guardian angels "who always behold the face of the Father who is in Heaven."

Was not that a wonderful thing to learn about those boys and girls and about you boys and girls who are reading this story now? That in that wondrous World of love and light and glory they are watching over you as if you were young princes and making delightful romantic plans for you?

I know the romantic dreams you youngsters have

of exciting adventures. How in your play you dress up and imagine yourselves princes and princesses and warriors and Indian chiefs and travellers and all sorts of things, and the stupid big people tell you such things will never happen.

Don't you believe them. Jesus said that in that World above far more wonderful and exciting things are planned for you. And they will all come true one day. All the lovely adventures that you dream of are not half as exciting as the adventures that will come to you some day in that World. Some of your comrades who have died and gone there are in the midst of those wonders now. Oh, you are pretty wonderful beings, you boys and girls.

Jesus just loved to tell things like that about that kindly World, so different from what people thought, so deeply interested in this poor world down here. It is because of that deep interest, He said, that I have come down to tell you the good news about our Kingdom and the Father's love for you, and to help you to get to it yourselves by and by.

Jewish house with a chamber on the roof.

III

BEFORE HE CAME

P EOPLE had been a long time living in this world before Jesus came. I don't know why He did not come earlier, for I know surely that this poor world always needed Him. But I know there must have been some good reason. And I know that long before they thought of Him He had been thinking of them and planning to come to them.

You know that our Bible has two parts, the Old Testament, which belongs to the time before He came, and the New Testament, which belongs to the time after He came. And in that Old Testament before He came we can read of things happening which were really to prepare for His coming, though the people who did those things did not know that at the time.

For instance, a long time before He came we read of a great shepherd camp in a hot Eastern land, and ignorant people who worshipped idols, and a thoughtful boy named Abram, who was puzzling himself thinking about the idols and about God. The Jews had some queer stories about that boy. That one day he went into the idols' room and smashed some of them with a big club and put the club into the hands of the big idol at the back. By and by his father came in a rage about his broken gods. "Who broke my gods?" he cried. And the boy said: "Father, look at the big idol with the club." "How could a wooden image do that?" cried his father. "Well, father," said the boy, "if these gods cannot do anything, why should we pray to them?"

They said, too, that he used to lie in the fields puzzling to find God. When he saw the glorious sun lightening the world, he would wonder, Can this be God? When he saw the moon sailing in the midnight sky he thought, Can that be God? But the sun passed away every evening and the moon vanished at dawn and the boy said, No, these are not God. I must still seek for the God who made all things.

These stories are not in the Bible so I don't know if they are true or not. But all the rest of the stories about him are in the Bible and we believe that they are all true. Evidently the boy was thinking hard and God put it into his mind when he grew up that he should go away from that land of idols and start a new life in a land that God would show him. So a new people grew up in that new land that we call Palestine and became a nation. They were called Hebrews or Jews. They were kept by themselves and trained to learn real religion, and God told Abram, perhaps in a dream, that through this new people one day all the families of the earth should be blessed.

Then among these Jews God put it into the minds of prophets and holy men that some Great One was some day to come, and they wrote down strange things about Him which God had put into their minds, such as this: "He shall be called Wonderful, Counsellor, the Mighty God, the Everlasting Father, the Prince of Peace, and of His government there shall be no end." And again: "Surely He hath borne our griefs and carried our sorrows. He is wounded for our wickedness and bruised for our sins and by His stripes we shall be healed."

I don't think the people understood what all this meant, but at any rate it set them thinking and wondering and expecting. It was preparing the world for the coming of Jesus. But for hundreds of years things went on as before. Nothing happened. God still kept silence.

At last one day "in the fulness of the time" God sent forth His Son! Jesus came. Born into the world as a little helpless baby! Should you ever have thought that the Lord of Heaven would come in that simple way?

IV

THE ANGEL'S MESSAGE

HERE is the story of how Jesus came.

Of course I had known this story since I was a child, but somehow, because it was in the Bible, I had a queer child notion that the place where these things happened was somewhere away out of the world. But as I grew up I knew better—that I could get into a train in my own town and then into a ship and sail away to the place where Jesus had lived long ago. All my life I had wanted to go. But I could not get away. But in beginning to write this story for you I felt that I must go and see the place for myself, and try to see in my mind the things as they happened.

So I started to sail from Canada across the ocean. I sailed past England and after many days came to the sunny Mediterranean Sea. (Look in the map for that.) Then at the far end of that great sea I saw before me the shores of Palestine, and landed in Jesus' country. There I travelled about with Jesus' story always in my mind, walking where Jesus had walked long ago, seeing what Jesus had seen. And the story became very real to me,

13

until at times I felt as if I were back in those wonderful old days with Jesus and His friends.

You know that on earth He was always called Jesus of Nazareth. Well, one day I was up among the hills of Galilee in Nazareth, the village where He lived the most of His life, where He had played as a child in the village street and worked in the carpenter's shop to support His mother; the village where His mother had lived as a girl. And there, walking in the very streets where Jesus had walked, I was thinking of what happened there 1,900 years ago.

What I saw was only a plain little town on the hillside, but the lovely memories of the places made it all-wonderful for me. The shabby little street was wonderful to me because Jesus had walked there, and the Nazareth boys on the roads set me picturing that Nazareth Boy of old walking on those self-same roads. There is a carpenter's shop there where a carpenter was making furniture and cattle yokes for the people, and near it is an old village well which has existed for ages and which must have been the very same well from which His mother drew the water for her home.

I felt as if I were back in the old Nazareth with the carpenter's shop in the village street and a strong country carpenter working at his bench with saw and chisel and hammer, making chairs and tables and cattle yokes for the country people, with the happy thought in his heart of his coming marriage and the home that he was preparing for his young bride. His name was Joseph. Somewhere down the village before me lived the girl whom he loved, Mary the daughter of Anne, a simple country girl working in her home, spinning and breadmaking and drawing water from the village well with the other girls in the evening.

It all seemed so real to me as I moved on to the well, that very same well, and watched the village girls filling their stone water-pots as those other girls did long ago when Mary was with them. I could imagine her there laughing and talking with the others, a girl gracious and modest, with a beautiful face to match her beautiful soul.

And I thought of Joseph the carpenter who loved her. He was older than she was, and I am sure he loved to watch her passing and to dream of their coming life together and to meet her in the evenings after his work and tell her of his plans and hopes. I feel sure they sometimes talked of greater things too. They were not careless lovers thinking only about themselves. They were religious people who loved God. Joseph, we are told, was "a righteous man," and Mary was a thoughtful, loving-hearted girl, fit to be chosen for God's great purpose.

Surely they would sometimes talk of what many religious Jews were thinking just then—the Great Hope of Israel, the Great Someone who was some day to come. And I could imagine the girl going home down that street after these meetings to pray for her lover's life and her own, and the Great World above listening to her prayers and thinking of their wonderful secret, the wonderful surprise they were preparing for her and for the world.

Of course she knew nothing about it. She never thought in her village home of the excitement above the bright blue sky, where the glorious inhabitants of that World above were preparing just then for their Lord's visit to this earth. But already some of them were preparing to come down and tell her. So the quiet days passed in Nazareth. Then—one night at her prayers— came suddenly on the girl a stirring of her whole being, a feeling of awe and wonder, and a lovely white angel stood before her with his message from the World above:—

"HAIL THOU THAT ART HIGHLY FAVORED
THE LORD IS WITH THEE."

And as she bowed there, frightened and astonished, came to her the tremendous message that the great hope of Israel, the hope of the long ages was to be fulfilled at last.

"FEAR NOT MARY, THOU HAST FOUND FAVOR WITH GOD.
FOR BEHOLD THOU SHALT CONCEIVE AND BRING FORTH A SON
AND THOU SHALT CALL HIS NAME JESUS.
OF HIS KINGDOM THERE SHALL BE NO END.
WHEREFORE THAT HOLY ONE THAT SHALL BE BORN OF THEE
SHALL BE CALLED THE SON OF GOD."

Did ever any other girl in the whole world get such a surprise as that! How could she sleep that night! How could she bear alone in her heart that exciting secret!

The angel had told her that another baby boy was coming to her cousin Elizabeth, the wife of a country priest down in the south country, the hills of Hebron, and that this boy was to prepare the way for Jesus. We shall hear a good deal about this other boy later on. So Mary, all wondering and excited, hurried away to tell Elizabeth and to talk with her about God's great plans for their boys. Then with the great wonder in her heart she came home to Nazareth to wait.

Two rather exciting things happened soon after. The first was her marriage day, when she became the wife of Joseph the carpenter and went to her new home beside the carpenter's shop. Joseph knew the great secret of the Angel's message and the Divine Child that was to be born of her. And scarce was she settled in her new home when one day the royal messengers went through the villages declaring the Emperor's orders that there should be what we call a Census, such as we have in our own country every ten years, to find out how many people there are in the country and to learn all about them. They were all to go back to their own towns where they were born and write down their names in the big Government book. So Joseph had to go a three days' journey to his native town Bethlehem, the town where King David had lived in olden days. And he took Mary with him. That is how it happened that "Jesus was born in Bethlehem of Judea in the days of Herod the King."

V

HOW JESUS CAME

AS I thought there in Nazareth about that ancient story, and how Joseph and Mary started on their journey to Bethlehem, I thought I would go to Bethlehem too, and see the very place where Jesus was born long ago. So I started from Nazareth in the early morning down the road where they had gone, 100 miles of hills and valleys where great things had happened long before their day in Old Testament stories, and I arrived in Bethlehem on Christmas Day, on Jesus' birthday!

Bethlehem is far down in the south, about five miles from Jerusalem. (Look at the map.) Those last five miles as I came near to Bethlehem were very interesting to me. For I could see in my mind that day long ago, when on that very bit of road was passing a straggling procession of travellers for the Census, some on foot, some on donkeys and camels, and amongst them a young countrywoman wearily riding, with her husband beside her leading the ass. And all around were more of the interesting places where things had happened in the Old Testament stories. Joseph, of course, knew all about them. He had walked and played all around there when he was a boy. And I think he would point them out to Mary as they passed.

As I thought of Joseph pointing them out to Mary I looked around to see them for myself. And I saw just where Joseph and Mary were looking at that day, where Ruth gleaned in the fields of Boaz, and where David, the shepherd boy, was minding his sheep that day when the lion and the bear came after them. That hollow to the right near the village is the place where the three brave men had risked their lives to bring David a drink of water from the well of Bethlehem. Here beside the road I saw Rachel's tomb, that spot sacred to all Jews where the light of Jacob's life went out that day when, as he says, "Rachel died by me in the land of Canaan, and I buried her by the roadside on the way to Ephrath" (which is Bethlehem).

Now they come to the white houses of Bethlehem and Joseph must hurry to find rest and shelter for his companion. These last few miles had been very tiring for her. I suppose he expected to stay with old friends in his native town. But the place was crowded with travellers for the Census. No place anywhere, not even in the inn.

Poor Joseph did not know where to go. At last he came on a stable in one of the caves with asses and camels tied up for the night, and there he found an empty stall and piled up a bed of hay and brought in his poor tired young wife to rest. And there that night in her loneliness and pain, with no kind woman to help her, her baby was born. "She brought forth her Son and wrapped Him in swaddling clothes"—there was no one else to do it—and laid Him in the manger with the cattle around Him for His first infant sleep. That is how the Lord from Heaven entered this world that first Christmas night.

Did ever a baby enter this world more humble and helpless! And somehow I think we love Him the better for it. One would think that if the Lord of Heaven should humble Himself to come down to earth, at any rate we should expect Him to be born in a palace with princesses around Him and high priests in attendance. I think I love Him best this way, a helpless winsome little baby whom nobody noticed, as if trusting Himself to us, wanting us to be fond of Him.

That is the tremendous thing, the lovely, wonderful, joyous thing which happened that Christmas night when "Jesus was born in Bethlehem of Judea in the days of Herod the King." And because of it in all the ages since, the thoughts of the whole Christian world turn every year at Christmas time to that little town. For nineteen hundred years past from all over the world, Christian travellers have been crowding every year to the little town of Bethlehem to see the place where Jesus was born.

> O come, all ye faithful, joyful and triumphant,
> O come ye, O come ye to Bethlehem;
> > Come and behold Him
> > Born the King of angels;

> O come, let us adore Him,
> O come, let us adore Him,
> O come, let us adore Him,
>   Christ the Lord.

In their loving reverence they have built a big church over the place, a big, ugly church which really spoils the whole picture. I wish they had let it alone, though I cannot help feeling with them in their desire to do honor to their dear Lord. But as I thought of the vast crowds, the great ones and the humble ones who have kept His birthday there for nineteen hundred years, I could not help thinking of His first lonely little birthday to which nobody troubled to come.

But that thought passed as I came out of the great church and saw in the sunny plain below the Field of the Shepherds with its wonderful story. It was not true, after all, that nobody troubled to come to His birthday.

For if princesses and high priests did not come to His birthday, there were visitors a thousand times greater who came. Just as He opened His eyes in that shabby old stable, suddenly came the distant sound of music sweeter than ever heard on earth, and outside over the stable and over the fields around the air was full of lovely white angels rejoicing and singing glad songs of welcome. For near by in the pasture fields under the stars, the Bible says, "There were shepherds abiding in the fields keeping watch over their flocks by night"— rough-looking shepherds in their loose cloaks sitting around the fire which they had built to keep them warm and to frighten away the wolves. Just common ordinary shepherds at their common ordinary work.

I don't know why anything wonderful should happen to them. I think that very likely they were religious shepherds talking, perhaps, and wondering about the prophecies in their Bible about the Great One who was some day to come from Heaven. Then as they sat looking up into the deep blue sky, spotted all over with glittering stars, suddenly there was a glory in the sky above them like what you sometimes see at evening in a glorious sunset. And as they sprang to their feet, pointing to the sky, they were gazing at a lovely angel with wide outstretched wings sailing down the sky— they were listening to the sweetest voice ever heard on earth. "Fear not," said he, "for, behold, I bring you good tidings of great joy, which shall be to all people. For unto you is born this day in the city of David a Saviour, which is Christ the Lord."—"And suddenly there was with the angel a multitude of the heavenly host praising God and saying, Glory to God in the highest and on earth peace, good-will to men!"

> It came upon the midnight clear,
>   That glorious song of old,
> From angels bending near the earth
>   To touch their harps of gold;
> Peace on the earth, good-will to men
>   From heaven's all-gracious King;
>   The world in solemn stillness lay
> To hear the angels sing.

The poor shepherds, of course, were astonished and frightened. They did not know at first what it all meant. But we know. And we know who those lovely white angels were. They were the people of Jesus' world beyond the sky, who had been watching for years while their world was preparing for Jesus to go down to earth, and now, when the time had come, they broke through in their gladness to rejoice over the world to which their Lord had come.

I think now, as we close this chapter, you might read over in your Bible that little story of the angels (Luke ii. 8-14), and try to picture it in your minds and try to think why the angels were so glad for us and why we should be glad for ourselves that the Son of God came down to visit our world on that first Christmas night long ago.

ONE OF OURSELVES

I am thinking of that helpless little baby lying in his mother's lap, smiling into his mother's face, kicking his little heels about, not able to do anything for himself nor caring to do anything, just a little helpless baby like one of ourselves.

And as I look and wonder I begin to see the lovely thing he has done, the lovely meaning of Jesus coming to us. He might have come as a compassionate stranger, an outsider looking down in pity and saying, "You poor people, I pity you, I am sorry for you and I want to help you." But Jesus said, "No; I am not going to be an outsider, I am coming right into their lives, coming right into the family as one of themselves."

That is why the little baby is there in his mother's lap. That little baby is the brother of all little babies. The growing child is the brother of all other children. You bigger boys and girls are the brothers and sisters of Jesus. The carpenter is the comrade of all the working men, bearing his troubles, sweating at his work just like the others. He is no stranger, just the elder brother of the family.

Just as you in your own family would love to see

your brothers and sisters happy and would be troubled at any bad thing happening to any of them, so with Jesus in the great human family He was born into. They were His brothers and sisters. He took the care of them all on His shoulders. He wanted His brothers and sisters to be happy and good. He wanted to help them up to God. He loved them. He cared for them. He cared so much that at last He laid down His life for them. And then after He went back to Heaven He kept the family on His heart for ever. He was still their Elder Brother though He was the Lord of Heaven.

Now do you see the exquisitely lovely way that Jesus came to us, not as a Visitor, not as an Outsider, but as one of the family, that little baby that grew up amongst us as one of ourselves.

Of all the wonders in the story of Jesus, is there anything more wonderful than this, that the Lord of Heaven was born into our family One of ourselves!

Mary's well in Nazareth.

THE SECOND BOOK

*How He grew up as a Boy in Nazareth
and afterwards worked at a carpenter's
bench to support His widowed mother.*

Nazareth

I

HIS BOYHOOD IN NAZARETH

AFTER that wonderful Christmas night, when the angels had gone back into Heaven leaving their Lord behind them here to start His human life as a little baby, we see but little of the Divine Child. There is a story which I don't quite understand about Wise Men from the East following a star and coming to worship Him. They thought the new-born Child was to be King of the Jews. And the wicked King Herod got frightened at their questions, for he thought this Child might take away his kingdom.

So he tried to find Him, and when he could not he sent soldiers down to kill all the little baby boys in Bethlehem, hoping to kill Jesus. That was an awful night for the poor mothers of Bethlehem. But the Child Jesus was not there, for Joseph and Mary had warning and had fled away with Him into Egypt, and there they stayed till the cruel old King was dead. By and by they got back to their old home in Nazareth beside the carpenter's shop, and there in that little mountain village Jesus was reared up.

So we come back to Nazareth. How we should love to know the story of Jesus' childhood in Nazareth, all the delightful things that mothers tell about their children and, as He grew older, all the boy life with His comrades, the games and play and excursions together that boys love to think about. One feels disappointed that the Bible does not tell us that story. Perhaps because the writers had not known Him as a boy. Perhaps because they had so much more important things to tell. Except for one thing that happened when He was twelve years old we are only told, "the Child grew and waxed strong, filled with wisdom; and the grace of God was upon Him."

And yet I feel that you are right in wishing to know about His life when He was about your own age. We like to know all we can about anyone that we really care for. And I think I know enough to picture His boyhood in my mind and help you to see it. For I know that He grew up like any ordinary Jewish boy and I know how other Jewish boys grew up in Nazareth.

So first I look at Nazareth as I saw it that day when I went up the hills of Galilee. Except for some changes in the houses of the town, the whole scene remains very much as Jesus saw it every day.

I see that little mountain town when Jesus lived there nestling white against the dark hills behind. I see those narrow, crooked streets that He saw, and the houses outside among the fields and gardens, and the vineyards on the terraced hills, and the green valleys bright in the springtime with lily and larkspur and dogrose and white anemone and all the lovely wild flowers of Northern Palestine in the springtime. There are the children playing in the streets and the girls in the evening at the village well, and out on the roads the country people in their queer dresses who, many of them, knew the Boy and were fond of Him. And the birds of the air that He often talks about; many of them birds that we know ourselves, the lark and the thrush and the robin and the crowds of common sparrows that He says God takes notice of, though He says you could buy them in the Nazareth market at two for a farthing. There I see the very mountain paths of His long walks, and the hill behind the town where on clear days He could see Mount Tabor and Mount Hermon and the mountains of Gilboa, where Saul and Jonathan died in that famous battle of Gilboa, and the highlands of Galilee spread out like a map, and far away the dark waters of the Mediterranean Sea.

That is Nazareth, His home. That is the boy world of Jesus which He thought of so often in later days. In the carpenter's cottage in one of these streets He lived, a natural human boy in a natural human family. In these fields and crooked streets He played with His comrades. On these mountain paths He walked and thought great thoughts as He grew up.

I think it must have been a wonderful time for His mother—often rather a puzzling time. You see, she knew what other people did not know. Just think of her listening to His childish talk and teaching Him His prayers and watching as He played with other boys or swept up the shavings in the carpenter's shop—and all the time with the wondering thought in her mind of the great things which the angel had told her.

Shall I tell you what used to puzzle me when I was young? I wonder if it puzzles you. How could these things be if she thought of Him as God from Heaven? How could she ever train Him up as her child and teach Him and tell Him to do things? How could He ever grow up as a natural human boy with other boys?

I can see now, as I study my Bible more carefully, that she did not yet think of Him as God. She only learned that great secret later. She knew that He came from Heaven. She knew that He was the Great One whom God had sent to help the world. But I am sure she did not understand till long afterwards the full meaning of the angel's message—the tremendous secret that He who came from Heaven as a little child was actually the Lord from Heaven Himself.

I don't think even the Child Himself at first understood who He was or thought of Himself as God. It was only as He grew up that He remembered and knew. It was meant that He should grow up as a natural human boy, that He should play with His comrades as a boy like themselves. I don't know what strange thoughts might sometimes come to Him, visions, perhaps, in His dreams of some world of light and beauty that He seemed dimly to remember. I only know that He felt Himself a natural boy like you.

All this is very hard for you to understand. But you cannot help that. The whole story of Jesus is hard to understand—that God became Man and lived with men for thirty years that they might, in some degree, get to know Him and understand Him and love Him.

II

SOME PICTURES OF HIS BOYHOOD

NOW I am seeing pictures in my mind of that Nazareth childhood. If you shut your eyes and think hard you can make those pictures with me. I see His mother at night putting her child to bed, teaching Him His prayers, and telling Him what she knew about God, and always with that thought in her mind of what the angel had said to her.

Then I think of the Boy, six years old, going to the village school with His companions. I see them, not sitting at a school desk like yours, but seated in a half-circle on the floor, as Eastern children sit while the teacher taught the lesson. I wonder what sort of man was that village rabbi who had the teaching of Jesus. Was he a stupid old man? Was he a wise, thoughtful man, who knew and understood children?

The American poet Longfellow was once making this picture in his mind, as I am doing now, of Jesus at school and of His teacher:—

"Come hither, Judas Iscariot,
Say if thy lesson thou hast got
From the rabbinical book or not.

*　　*　　*　　*　　*　　*

And now, little Jesus the carpenter's son,
Let us see how Thy task is done," etc.

Nearly all the teaching was out of the Bible. Jewish writers tell us of children's little books, such as the Story of Genesis. The children learned by heart their "Shema" which is like our Creed. For hymns they learned the easy simple psalms just as you know them. For history lessons they had the story of what God did for their country in olden days. You can read in your Bible in the Old Testament the very history lessons that Jesus learned by heart. When He was older He learned to read them for Himself in His Bible. But you could not read them. They were in queer square big letters and He had to read them backward! Jewish books are all read backward. Here is a bit of one of His older lesson books which you can read backward as He did.

האָרֶץ	וְאֵת	הַשָּׁמַיִם	אֵת	אֱלֹהִים	בָּרָא	בְּרֵאשִׁית
earth the	and	heavens the		God	made	beginning the In

Now you can feel proud that you have learned a lesson in Hebrew. If any of your friends are inclined to boast of their cleverness you can quietly remark that you have been reading part of the Hebrew Bible to-day!

After school don't you like to think of Him "playing in the market-place"? It seems to bring Him so close to ourselves. Just think of it. Jesus, our blessed Lord in Heaven, the children's Lord and the children's Friend, once was a child and played at His merry games like you. Surely He would understand the feelings of children in school or at play, in happiness or in trouble. Nobody understands a child as Jesus does. I came one day on a delightful discovery—Jesus, as a man, remembering the games of His childhood.

In the child world of long ago they seemed to play the same sort of games and sing the same sort of rhymes as children do to-day. One often hears young children dancing in a ring and singing "London Bridge is broken down," or "Round and round the mulberry bush." Just like that you might have heard the Nazareth children long ago singing in their game of "Weddings and Funerals":

> "We have piped and ye *non rakedtoon,*
> We have mourned and ye *non arkedtoon.*"

And long afterwards Jesus remembered that little rhyme one day when He was preaching.[1] He was blaming the people for their foolishness. "You are just like a set of children," He said, "playing in the market-place and calling to each other:

> "We have piped and ye *non rakedtoon,*
> We have mourned and ye *non arkedtoon.*"

It means in English,

> "We have piped unto you and ye have not danced,
> We have mourned unto you and ye have not wept."

We cannot make it rhyme in English or in the Greek language of the New Testament, but it does rhyme in

[1] Luke vii. 32.

the language of the Nazareth children. It must have been the song of a children's game, and I shall never again hear village children singing in the market-place without thinking of that rhyme and the child Jesus at play.

I think those little memories of His childhood often came back at other times too when He was a man. In one of His sermons He told of a woman making bread and mixing leaven into three measures of meal. I have often wondered why He said *three measures;* probably it was because that was the amount His mother used every week for her bread-making.

So I think of that mother making her bread and a little boy no higher than the bread-board running His fingers through the meal and asking His childish questions as to what His mother was doing and why she was mixing leaven in it. I think that childish memory was in His mind when He told of the woman mixing leaven in three measures of meal. We older people have often little childish memories like that coming back in our minds.

By and by as He grew bigger I can picture Him in the older games of boyhood, or tramping over the hills with some of the more thoughtful boys. I wonder what they talked about.

I remember a little story I once heard of Jesus and the Nazareth boys. It is not in the Bible. I don't know where it comes from, but it is a true picture of what Jesus was like. We learn afterwards that He could always see any little good in people whom others thought all bad.

This story tells that the boys one day saw a little dog dead by the roadside. "What an ugly little brute," they said. "What a nasty smell!" Then young Jesus came up. "Oh, what lovely white teeth," said He. "They are whiter than ivory." You see He just saw at once the only beautiful thing in that ugly little dog. That was just like Him when He met people afterwards that other people thought were altogether bad. If there was any little bit of good in them He would see it at once. He always looked for the good in everybody.

One caution I must give you before this chapter closes. We have been thinking of Our Lord in His childhood, in home and school and play as a natural human boy like ourselves, not yet thinking who He really was or the reason why He was here on earth. But we must not make too free with our thoughts of Him. We must always keep in mind who He really was. I suppose the other Nazareth boys, His comrades whom He played with, thought of Him as just one of themselves, braver perhaps and better and more pleasant as a comrade—one who never did or thought anything mean or cowardly or unkind. But still an ordinary Nazareth boy. They knew no better.

But we know better and must always reverently keep in mind that this was really the Lord from Heaven growing up to bless the whole world for ever.

God was very close in the heart of that Divine Boy. He must always have felt happy in the presence of the

Father in Heaven. In all the enjoyment of play with His comrades He would feel that the Father in Heaven was looking on them and loving them and liked to see them happy in their play. All children ought to feel that. But nobody would feel it as He did because He knew. And all the world around He would feel as His Father's world. He saw God everywhere. Everything was teaching Him His lovely happy religion.

I think of Him out on the hillside seeing God's green hills and pleasant streams, and God's sun coming to light the world and sinking at evening in crimson glory into the Great Sea; seeing the Father's birds and flowers and beasts, and delighting in them and loving them, and feeling that the Father also delighted in them and loved them. In all His teaching afterwards He makes us feel this. He tells us that God is behind it all, interested in it all. That God loves the little lambs sporting in the fields. That God watches the poor sheep going astray. God feeds the birds of the air which toil not neither do they spin. God sees the young sparrow fallen out of the nest. He clothes the grass of the field. He paints for His pleasure the wild flowers of the hillside so that "Solomon in all his glory was not arrayed like one of these."

Surely Jesus, who knows our child-world so well, would like us all to have that same happy childlike religion with the thought of that kindly Father so near to us always. Surely Jesus was a happy Child in that free, simple boyhood in Nazareth before the thought of the world's sin and pain began to press upon His heart. So gradually humanly, as the Bible says, "the Child grew and waxed strong in spirit, and the grace of God was upon Him, and daily He grew in wisdom and stature and in favor with God and Man."

Carrying water from the well.

III

WHEN HE WAS TWELVE

A RE any of you yet twelve years old? Think of some boy of twelve whom you know and like. When Jesus was twelve there comes the one only story in the Bible about His boyhood. I wonder why it was told. I will tell you my guess about the reason later on. We read that Joseph and Mary went up to Jerusalem every year to the Feast of the Passover, and when He was twelve years old He went up with them.

The Passover was a great religious festival like our Easter. It was to remind the Jews how God had saved their children from a great danger long ago when they were slaves in Egypt. All religious Jews all over the world looked forward to it every year and would try to come back to Jerusalem for this great festival. Children did not go. But when a Jewish boy was twelve he became a "son of the Law." It was something like our Confirmation, or what happens in any religious body when a child is received as a full member of his Church. Jesus' childhood was over and He could now go to the great festivals with the grown-up men.

Surely a wonderful day for this Nazareth boy! His

first Passover that He had been looking forward to for years!

Cannot you imagine the excitement of a young country boy, who had never seen anything of the great world, starting off on this delightful excursion on the long road with the Holy City of His dreams at the end of it. Last year I travelled on that road from Nazareth to Jerusalem. I, too, had never seen Jerusalem. I was quite excited over it as we travelled over the hundred miles of Jesus' road and saw all the country that He saw that day, and strained our eyes to catch the first sight of Jerusalem on the hills. So I can almost see Him on that pleasant excursion.

I see Him that morning setting out from the carpenter's cottage with the band of Nazareth neighbors in their best clothes. I see Him travelling down the Nazareth road to the plains, watching the new groups of people that joined their procession at every crossroad, passing some of the famous places told of in His history lessons, thinking of Elisha as they rested at Shunem, passing by Gibeah, the birthplace of King Saul, joining in the chant of the Psalms about Jerusalem as they caught the first sight of the Holy City in the distance. Above all, He was going to see Jerusalem, the Capital of His nation, the City of God. Surely, for Him, a day to be remembered.

And then when He got to Jerusalem! All that week the wonder and reverence would grow. Think of His feeling as He entered the stately temple, the house of the Father, the centre of Israel's worship all the world over. Think how His young heart would be stirred as He saw the vast crowds that had come to the Passover, more than a million of religious Jews from every nation under Heaven, crowding the streets, camping like a great army along the hills and plains outside, all come together with one great purpose—to worship the Father in His Holy Temple!

Think of Him again that solemn Passover night, when each family or group of families held in some upper room their own private feast of the Passover, when the lamb that was slain and the unleavened bread were placed on the table and the youngest boy present, probably Jesus Himself, had to ask the question in their Jewish prayer-book, "What mean ye by this service?" and the oldest man at the feast solemnly replied: "It is the sacrifice of the Lord's Passover, who passed over the houses of the children of Israel and delivered our houses." I don't suppose Jesus knew yet that these ceremonies had any connection with Himself, that the "lamb that was slain" at the Passover feast was to point to Him the "Lamb of God who should take away the sins of the world." But you can see how the Boy would wonder and get excited about it all.

Something else also happened that week which evidently was important. At Passover time the great Rabbis, the learned teachers of the nation, used to sit on the Temple terrace to teach. It was simple, easy teaching. Anybody might come. Anybody might ask questions. And one day the Boy, straying through the beautiful Temple courts with the wonder and excitement in His eyes, suddenly opened a gate and found Himself on the terrace! In a moment mother and friends and everything were forgotten. Here was His young mind longing for knowledge that He could not get from the ignorant old rabbi in Nazareth. There were the greatest teachers of the nation, the men who knew!

All that evening He stands eagerly listening, and at night when the Temple was closed and He set off to find His friends the little country boy got lost in the streets of the strange city. I suppose He slept that night on somebody's doorstep. I suppose some kind woman was good to the lost child and gave Him food. Next morning He is back again listening, thinking. And sometimes He asks eager questions. At last the great Rabbis begin to notice Him and get interested, and then begin to "wonder at His understanding and answers."

I wish we knew the questions that He asked. I wish we knew all that He was thinking that day. It seems that it was His mother that told this story to St. Luke, who writes it in the Bible, and she only came in at the end and did not know. She came in frightened and worried. They had been searching three days for the lost Boy, imagining all sorts of terrible things happening to Him, and now she finds Him safe and interested and excited, not thinking at all, it seems, of her and her anxiety. How little she knew of the great thoughts stirring in the heart of her Child!

"My Son," she asks, "why have You done this to us? For three days we have been seeking and sorrowing." In His answer we have the very *first recorded words* of Jesus. "Why, mother, how is it that you are surprised?

Should not you expect to find Me in the house of My Father, about My Father's business?"

Was not that a startling answer for a young boy of twelve? I think it startled even His mother. And it sets me thinking and guessing. I told you I was trying to guess why this one story alone should be told of all the life of His boyhood. You might try to guess with me. Do you think it might be because there was just beginning to dawn on Him the thought of who He really was and why He was here on earth; that He was just beginning to feel Himself somehow different from those about Him, from the boys He had played with and the parents who had reared Him up? We are only guessing. But I know God was very close to the heart of that Boy, and I feel that all these wonders of the Passover week would set Him thinking hard. So maybe my guess is right. What do you think about it?

I think His mother must have felt something like this, for the Bible says "they understood not the saying which He spake to them. But His mother kept all these things in her heart." She could not understand. And the Boy had to think out His great thoughts alone. And He was only twelve. I think it must have been a bit lonely for Him.

Now the Passover is ended—the excitement is all over. Everybody is going home. You know how dull and flat it seems after holidays or other exciting times. You have to go back home to school and lessons and all the common everyday life. If you had had all the great thoughts and great happenings and excitement of that week that Jesus had you would probably feel it still more. It would be so much pleasanter to stay in the city, and in that glorious temple to learn great things and do great things "about His Father's business." But for Jesus at present the dull village life was "His Father's business." For you, too, at present the quiet life of home and school is the Father's business that you are to do for Him to train you for bigger things by and by.

So I read that He went home with His parents and came to Nazareth and was subject to them. He was only twelve and the simple home life was no doubt the best preparation for His future. So He was to go back to the dull village life and the home duties and the carpenter's shop. He was to grow up in that lone little mountain town, unnoticed and unknown, thinking His great thoughts, doing His common work, until the time came that He should go out into the world and do the great things for us.

So the Boy passes out of our sight down the Nazareth road on His way home and we see Him no more and know nothing more about Him for several years.

IV

JESUS THE CARPENTER

NOW we take a long step forward. Eighteen years have passed before we look again at the home in Nazareth. The Divine Boy has grown to be a man. The good Joseph the carpenter is dead, and the lonely widow has sobbed out her grief in the arms of her beloved Son. Ah, it was good to have Him near her in the day of her sorrow, good to have Him to stand by her in all the lonely years to come until as He was leaving this world, from the agony of the Cross, He gave her into the care of His closest friend and bade him take care of her in her old age as a son would care for his mother. We shall read about that later.

Evidently He had to work for His widowed mother's support at the trade that Joseph had taught Him. "Is not this the carpenter, the Son of Mary?" said the Nazareth neighbors when He came back one day later on a visit to His native village. So we think of Jesus as He grew to be a man, working as a country carpenter, supporting His widowed mother.

Think of the Son of God in His lowly humility. A workman at his trade, a carpenter earning money. He made ploughs and cattle yokes for the Nazareth farmers. And you may be sure they were good ploughs and cattle yokes. And so He taught mankind for ever what a fine thing is honest work in the sight of God. In His day, as in our day, rich people looked down on a working man. "He is only a carpenter," said the stupid Nazareth people. We must never think like that. For Jesus as a working man makes one feel that all honest work is a noble thing in the sight of God. I once read an old carpenter's thoughts about it:—

> "I don't know right where His shed may have stood,
> But often as I've been a-planing my wood
> I've took off my hat just when thinking of He
> At the same work as me,
> And I warrant He felt a bit proud like I've done
> At a good job begun.
> So I comes right away by mysen with the Book,
> And I turns the old pages and has a good look
> At the text I have found that tells me as He
> Were the same trade as me."

I always think of that workshop as a friendly sort of place, for I am sure that His neighbors honored and liked that young carpenter, and would come to talk to Him while He worked. And I like to think that children were not discouraged from coming into that workshop among the shavings. For they surely liked Jesus. "He was in favor with God and in favor with men," says the Bible. And we are sure He was in favor with children. We know that later on He loved to have children about Him and they loved to be with Him. And no doubt He had the habit of telling them stories, for He was always telling stories in His later life, and we can hardly believe that He never did it before. And surely the children would learn from the stories in that workshop more about God's love and care than from all the religious teaching of the village school.

Now the time was coming near that He should go out to His great work in the world. We could never understand the high thoughts in His mind as He worked at His bench all day and went out for long walks in the evening on the Nazareth hills, thinking about the great mystery of His future, or staying on the hills as He used to do in later days "continuing all night in prayer to God."

So the quiet years rolled on till "Jesus began to be about thirty years old." Then at last the time was come. He must go out into the world to His great life work "for us men and for our salvation."

That year there was keen excitement all over the land. He heard everyone talking of a new prophet, a queer rough prophet in a hairy robe, who was preaching and saying strange things down in the wild country in the South. It was 500 years since any great prophet had come. So naturally they were excited about this prophet. "Who are you?" they asked him. "Are you the Christ? Are you the Great One coming from Heaven that our Bible says is to come?"

"No," he said. "I am not that Great One. I am not the Christ. But He is coming and coming soon. I am only the poor messenger before His face who shall prepare the way before Him."

Of course the Nazareth people were excited about this news. The farmers in the field, the girls at the well, the men who came into the carpenter's shop were talking about this mysterious prophet in the South and the startling things he was saying about Him who was to come. And Jesus heard and understood. One night He laid down His carpenter's tools for the last time and closed the carpenter's shop. It was the end of all His long years of waiting. "Then Jesus arose and went from Galilee to the Jordan to John, to be baptized of him."

THE THIRD BOOK

*How He went out to His life work.
How He was baptized and fought a
great battle with the Devil, and how
John the Baptist died.*

I

HIS BAPTISM

I WONDER have you guessed who was this strange prophet of the wilderness who was startling the people, warning them about their sins and telling of the Coming One? Have you forgotten after the angel's visit, how the Blessed Virgin hurried away to that country clergyman's house among the beautiful hills to tell of her great secret to his wife Elizabeth, and that another baby boy was coming to Elizabeth who should by and by prepare the way for Jesus and His Kingdom? Now you know who was the Wilderness Prophet. He was called John the Baptizer. John the Baptist.

The two children, Jesus and John, were born within the same year. We have been learning what we could about the boyhood of Jesus. We know nothing at all about the childhood of this other boy. We think of him growing up an only child. A silent lonely boy without brothers or sisters or playmates, puzzling over the wonderful thing his father had told him, that he was "sent to prepare the way of the Lord." We think of him as a grown man, a lone hermit in the wilderness, wearing his rough robe of camel's hair and feeding on locusts and wild honey that he found in the woods. And all the time thinking of the great future before him and studying what his Bible said about the Great One who was to come. One feels sorry for him—always alone struggling with his thoughts, fighting his doubts, no one to encourage him, no one to praise him. He thought nothing of himself. "I am but a voice crying in the wilderness," he said. He sought nothing for himself, and he got nothing. He was just to hold the door open for others. He was to have no happy companionship with Jesus as others had. When others were rejoicing in the friendship of Jesus he was being murdered in a prison cell. That poor lonely prophet!

But God was with him. He could speak to God in his prayers. And he felt he was doing what God wished him to do, and that is a great comfort to any true man. So he went on preaching to the people and baptizing all who would turn from their sins. So they called him John the Baptizer, John the Baptist.

Now the whole countryside is up and excited. Crowds are coming from everywhere to the banks of the Jordan, men and women, townfolk and countryfolk, traders and tax-gatherers, soldiers and farmers, priests and rabbis, among them a young countryman that nobody knows, but we know Him, coming down the Nazareth road. Day after day He listened and watched them. Then one day, when the baptisms were over and the Baptist stood alone, Jesus alone walked out into the water! In a moment I see the prophet staring, startled and wondering. I hear the sudden question, "Who is it? Who is it?"—"I knew Him not," he says. I suppose he did not know whether the Coming One was already on earth or whether He would come suddenly from Heaven in power and great glory. But in that presence he felt moved to the depth of his being. Some great one surely this was who stood before him! And then—Jesus raised His eyes and looked him straight in the face. And then, in a moment, he knew! He knew! He whom he had dreamed of all those lonely years, straining his ears to catch the coming of His feet, the Christ, the hope of Israel, He is come!

Cannot you feel the intense excitement of the man, the awe and wonder in his heart! "Oh, how could I dare to baptize You. I am but a poor sinful man that should ask You to baptize me." But Jesus bade him go on. The Baptist laid his hands on Him and bowed Him beneath the water. And as He rose from the water a tremendous thing happened—something which neither of these two would ever forget. Suddenly to them both the Heavens opened and a vision like a Dove lighted upon Jesus and a voice was heard by them, a voice from Heaven. "This is My beloved Son, in whom I am well pleased!"

So the Lord Jesus entered on His great office and the Baptist knew of a certainty that he had found the Christ. After the Baptism he said solemnly to the people: "One is standing in the midst of you whom ye know not!"

The next time he saw Jesus he cried to those about him: "Behold the Lamb of God!"

The Jordan Valley.

II

HOW JESUS FOUGHT
HIS GREAT BATTLE
WITH THE DEVIL

NOW comes suddenly to us an extraordinary story, a dark, awful story, not easy to understand. Immediately after the Baptism the Bible says, "Then was Jesus led up by the Holy Spirit into the Wilderness to be tempted of the devil!" What can it mean? Try to think.

I see Jesus coming up out of the water all excited over the tremendous thing that had happened—the voice from Heaven, the knowledge of who He was, the thought of the great work for which He had come down from Heaven. Cannot you imagine how at such a time He would want to get away from people to be alone, to think, to make plans. I see Him passing through the crowd on the river bank, wandering away alone up the winding road into the hills, away into the wild desert land amongst the wild beasts. All night long He keeps going, forgetting all around Him, thinking only the wonderful thoughts that were filling His soul and making His plans for the future, when suddenly a horrible thing happens. Evil spirits in the air crowd in on Him, struggling, tempting, tormenting, trying to lead Him wrong! Think of the pure and holy Jesus in such horrible company!

There all alone for forty days, St. Luke says, He was led in the wilderness tempted of the devil. This is too hard for us to understand. Don't you think it means that the devil wanted to spoil His great life plans, to prevent Him from saving and blessing the world? At any rate, Jesus knew that He must face this terrible thing. He was led by the Holy Spirit into the wilderness to be tempted of the devil. So when it was a duty that He ought to face of course He faced it. But it must have been a horrible thing for Him. We can never know how horrible. Think of forty days of such terrible struggle and strain and excitement that He never thought of food, did not even notice that He was hungry. People in intense excitement often forget to eat.

Whether the devil came as a black angel of evil that He could see, we don't know; or whether he came as he sometimes comes to us in our little temptations. Did he ever come to you? Could you see him? No, but you know that he was there trying to make you do wrong. Probably he came like that to Jesus. We don't know. But whether he was visible or not, Jesus says he was the devil. Think of this when you feel the devil tempting you. A real wicked devil. Do not just say, "I feel wicked thoughts and desires," but say, "I am tempted of the devil like our Lord. I ought to rise up and fight him bravely in the strength which our Lord will give me."

Our temptations are small things, so small sometimes that we should be ashamed to let them conquer us; just to tell a lie, to be cross and tempered, to be selfish or disobedient. But these temptations of Jesus must have been something very awful, so awful that I suppose we could not understand them. We are only told a little bit at the end.

After that terrible strain of the forty days Jesus suddenly felt weak and fainting, nearly dying of hunger. And just then the devil whispered, "If You are really the Son of God turn these stones into bread!" Of course He could do it. He was the Lord from Heaven and could do anything. He had all power in Heaven and earth. But He only came to use these powers for us. He would not use them for Himself to make His own struggle easier. You see, He had come down to us on our level as a man, as our brother, and would take no advantage that we could not have. Like an armored knight of old, fighting beside his unarmored peasant soldiers, he puts away his armor and his shield and horse and fights on foot just like themselves. So Jesus would fight the devil just as you and I have to fight him, without any miracle to help us. He was tortured with hunger. His body was craving terribly for food. But Jesus says, "No, I ought not, I will not do this thing." So the devil was beaten that time.

Then the devil tried again. It is said that he took Jesus up to a pinnacle of the temple, the top of the great church steeple, and said to Him: "Now if You throw yourself down in the midst of the crowd below it will show how You trust God to take care of You, and people will see what a wonderful being You are and will follow

You in crowds and will do all the good things You want them to do. They are expecting wonderful miracles like that from You. So You will march out in triumph from the temple and escape all the pain and trouble of slowly winning men to follow You."

But Jesus' plan was very different. He wanted to win men not by miracles and wonders but by love; by showing them the affection and pain and self-sacrifice of God. If that would not win them nothing else would. It would be a hard, slow, painful road. It would mean for Himself suffering and death. But He would choose that hard road.

"No," He said, "I ought not, I will not do this thing."

So the devil was beaten again.

Then he tried once more. By his strange evil powers he took Jesus up to an exceeding high mountain and showed Him in a vision all the kingdoms of the world in a moment of time. A wonderful vision. The whole beautiful world lying before Him in the sunshine with its cities and palaces, its peoples, rich and grand and powerful and all bowing down in worship of God. A vision of the very thing that Jesus wanted. But how should He get it? "All these things I will give You," said the devil, "if You will bow down and worship me."

Then Jesus was angry. "Get away from Me!" He replies. "Get thee behind Me, Satan, for it is written in the Bible, Thou shalt worship the Lord thy God, and Him only shalt thou serve!"

Then the devil fled from Him, beaten again for the last time. Jesus had won all along the line. And behold, angels came and ministered unto Him.

Do you know what I think after reading this story? That maybe the devil is not half as strong as people think. I think he is like a big, cowardly bully that will run away if we fight him. You have seen a big coward bullying a small boy, and the small boy is too frightened to fight him. But sometimes if the small boy gets fierce and hits back, the bully will run away.

I think the devil is like that big bully. Would not it be a proud thing to make him run away? Whenever the devil attacks you to make you do wrong, just think how the Lord Jesus is looking to see whether you are going to be a coward and let him bully you or coax you, or whether you are going to hit back and say "No!" And always remember that Jesus, who fought that awful battle with him long ago, is greatly interested in your little battle with him and always standing by to help you.

The Wilderness

III

YOUNG JOHN
THE DISCIPLE'S STORY

ALL this time, while Jesus was away in His terrible struggle with the devil, John the Baptist has been teaching and baptizing by the river with the crowds around him. I suppose he often wondered where Jesus of Nazareth could have gone to. He had not seen Him for a whole six weeks and did not know what had happened to Him. Then one day suddenly he saw Jesus again as He was coming back from that awful wilderness. And so here comes a lovely story of a most interesting week, when the Baptist saw Jesus coming back from the wilderness and when Jesus first met the young comrades who were to be His disciples and apostles in the days to come. It is one of these young comrades himself who told it long afterwards when he was a very old man far away from his native land and wrote it in his new book (the Gospel of St. John).[2] He saw that St. Matthew and St. Mark and St. Luke had not written it in their books and I suppose he felt, "I must surely tell of those wonderful

[2]St. John, chap. i. 35 ff.

days when I first saw the face of my dear Lord." So in his book that he was writing about Jesus he sketches in his memories of that week after the Temptation. And amongst all his memories one especially stands out, the precious memory of a certain afternoon at four o'clock fifty years before, the hour when he first met his beloved Lord.

He was a young fisherman from the Sea of Galilee and he and a few young comrades had taken a holiday to come and hear John the Baptist. One day as they talked with him, suddenly, down the hill path where He had disappeared six weeks ago, Jesus appeared walking towards them, a very tired Jesus, with the strain of those awful forty days showing on Him and the light of another world in His eyes. The Baptist recognizes Him at once. He had been wondering all the time where He had gone to. Now he eagerly points Him out to his young companions. "Behold the Lamb of God, Who taketh away the sins of the world! This is He that I have been telling you about. I saw the Holy Spirit descending on Him like a dove out of Heaven, and I have seen and bear witness that this is the Son of God."

That was young John the disciple's first sight of Jesus. Could he ever forget it! I call him young John the disciple. Do not confuse him in your minds with John the Baptist.

Then he goes on to tell how the next day in the afternoon he and his comrade Andrew were again talking with the Baptist, talking surely about Jesus, when again on the path below by the river Jesus passed.

"There He is again!" cried the Baptist; "the Lamb of God!" And the two young comrades could not resist the sudden craving in their hearts as they saw Jesus going away. Probably the Baptist encouraged them to go after Him. Down the path they followed after Him, shyly, timidly, awkwardly, half hoping, half fearing that He might speak to them. And Jesus, hearing the footsteps behind Him, turned round and saw them following. He knew their hearts. Kindly, encouragingly He asks them, "What seek ye?" The startled young countrymen hardly know what to say. "Master, where dwellest Thou?" Ah, Jesus knew what they wanted. "Come with Me," He said, and He took them to His poor little lodging and there they stayed all the evening with Him. John remembers so clearly, looking back over half a century. It was about the tenth hour, he says (four o'clock). It always helps us to imagine any remarkable event when we know at what time of the day or night it took place. He remembers the very hour. How could he ever forget!

Think what it meant to be all that evening alone with Jesus, sharing His simple supper, questioning Him, talking to Him easily and naturally as to a friendly comrade not much older than themselves. I think they almost forgot that He was some great person as they told Him of their life in the fishing boats and of the simple thoughts and wishes in their hearts. And I think He told them something of His plans and hopes and enthusiasms for the lovely Kingdom of God that He wanted to found in the world. And I should not wonder if He said to them before they parted: "Would you like to stand by Me some day and help?"

I am thinking of those two, Andrew and John, coming back that night under the starlight, their hearts stirring with wonder and enthusiasm and with a deep, reverent affection for their new friend. Aye, they would follow Him, follow Him to the death if He asked them. The whole world was changed for them that night. Earth was never the same again.

That was how Jesus got His first two comrades. Not by preaching to them and telling them He was God, or frightening them about the fate of sinners, but just by loving them and making friends with them, letting them know Him. Don't you think we should all want to be His friends if we got to know Him like that?

Then St. John's story goes on, "One of us two was Andrew, Simon Peter's brother." So delighted is Andrew over that evening with Jesus that he goes right off to find his brother. "Simon, we have found the Christ!" So he brought him to Jesus. That was how Simon Peter—the rash, blundering, affectionate Peter—came into the group, and in spite of all his faults became one of the truest, dearest friends that Jesus had. I think surely Andrew was glad that he had brought him. I think any of us who had got to know, as Andrew had, what Jesus was really like would want to bring our comrades to know Him.

Again John's story of that wonderful week goes on. He and Andrew and Peter have to go home to their work. They have been long enough away and the fishing boats are waiting for them on the Lake of Galilee. And they learn with delight that Jesus is starting to go North to Galilee the next day. He has to stop at the little town of Cana the day after to-morrow for a wedding. They, too, are invited to that wedding. So they all start off together that April morning when Palestine looks its loveliest, with the whole country covered with flowers. They crossed the Great White Road from the East, where the merchants from India and Persia would be passing with their bales of merchandise going to Europe.

Then they have a long tramp, over twenty miles, to get to Cana before evening. On the road they overtake one of their comrades, Philip, who comes from their village at home. I think Philip already knew the Lord Jesus. And he has a great friend in Cana named Nathaniel. He can hardly wait till he gets to Cana before hurrying off to find Nathaniel. "Oh, Nathaniel, listen! We have found Him whom Moses and the prophets told about in the Bible. He is called Jesus of Nazareth!"

Nathaniel would not believe him at first. He was a deeply religious man and knew from his Bible that some Great One should come, but he did not believe much in the wisdom of young Philip. He did not think it at all likely that the great Coming One should come from a carpenter's shop in the valley just over the hill. "Well, come and meet Him at any rate," said Philip. So Nathaniel came and the moment he looked into the eyes of Jesus he felt that strange attraction which all true hearts felt when they met Him. Then Jesus spoke to him as if He knew him already. "But how can You know me?" said Nathaniel. And Jesus answered, "I know all about you, Nathaniel. Before Philip called you, when you were praying under the fig tree this morning, I was looking at you."—"He knows even what I was thinking of this morning," said Nathaniel to himself. "He knows all about me." And in a moment Nathaniel believed on Him utterly. "Master, you are the Son of God, you are the King of Israel."

So already in these few days Jesus had won live eager young comrades who would die for Him if necessary. You will find their full names afterwards in the list of His apostles.

One day lately I went to see this little town of Cana where Nathaniel lived. It is a poor, shabby, ruined little place now, but I loved to look at it and to think of that interesting day long ago when Jesus walked into it with His five young friends.

IV

THE WEDDING IN
CANA OF GALILEE

YOU remember that Jesus stopped at Cana because He was invited to a wedding. St. John is continuing his story of that wonderful week that he remembered so well, his first week with Jesus. "Now the third day," he says, "there was a marriage in Cana of Galilee and the mother of Jesus was there. And Jesus also was invited and His disciples to the marriage."

I think it must have been a wedding in the family, for I see that the mother of Jesus is managing the wedding feast. Either the bride or the bridegroom was a cousin or relative of Jesus. I like to think of that little village bride with her white veil and the myrtle wreath in her hair, glad and proud because Jesus had come to her wedding. Probably she had known Him from childhood, for her home in Cana was only four miles away from the carpenter's shop at Nazareth. Perhaps she was one of the children to whom He used to tell stories in the carpenter's shop, and now she wanted her great Cousin whom she admired and loved to be present and to see her happiness and to bless her. You might think that Jesus, who was so great and who had such great thoughts and plans in His mind, would not waste time coming to a little country wedding. But Jesus came and I think He liked coming and I think these simple village people liked to have Him with them. Jesus made happiness wherever He came because He was so happy Himself.

You have seen pictures of Jesus with a sad countenance. That is all wrong. Of course He was sad sometimes, because His loving heart felt so deeply the sin and unhappiness around Him. But He could feel also the brightness and happiness of life, the beautiful world, the happy people, the pleasant friendships, the children rejoicing in their play, and the loving Father in Heaven looking on it all and loving it. And He knew that He was come to make all happier and better. He really enjoyed life. Nobody enjoyed life as Jesus did. He enjoyed every bit of it. He delighted in the birds and flowers and the lovely world. He delighted in little children. He enjoyed His friendships and could not bear to be without them. He could laugh pleasantly at weddings. He loved meeting people. He is constantly cheering up sorrowful people. Cheer up, He says over and over again. Cheer up. Be of good cheer!

Why, of course He was happy. The happiest people in the world to-day are those who are doing most for others, and the people who have joyous, trustful thoughts of God and the people who know that death only means birth into a fuller life. None of us could help being happy if we were like Him and knew what

He knew. Even when big troubles came, even the night before He was crucified, His last wish for the poor disciples was "that My joy may remain in you that your joy may be full."

I love to think about Jesus at that country wedding. That He did not think Himself too great to come, that He enjoyed being there, and that they enjoyed having Him. For I think it brings lovely happy thoughts of God for ourselves. Why? Because Jesus was God. So I learn the kindly nature of God. God likes weddings. God likes happiness. Watch Jesus at this wedding, happy, human, natural, sympathizing with the joy of young lovers in their marriage, and say to yourself, That is God, that is how God feels.

God, of course, cares most of all for goodness and nobleness of life, but God is not a sort of high clergyman interested only in our prayers and church services and not caring at all about our pleasures and laughter and games and amusements. He is interested in the birds and the beautiful flowers and the lambs skipping in the field and the children singing in the market-place and the boys and girls at their games and the mother's tender thought for her baby and the shy young bride meeting her bridegroom. God has given us beautiful music. God gave us humor and laughter to make things pleasant. I think He likes to see us laughing. I think that to set a group of people merrily, innocently laughing is doing the will of the Father who is in Heaven.

That is the lovely happy religion that Jesus wants us to have.

Now an awkward thing happened at the wedding feast. Somebody discovered that the wine had run short, and the poor bride and bridegroom felt that they would be shamed before their friends because they were too poor to provide properly for their feast. A proud, poor Galilean family would feel that deeply. And Jesus knew they would. He belonged to a very poor family Himself and He understood their feelings. In a moment He decided what to do. A week ago, at the Temptation, He had refused to turn stones into bread to relieve His own hunger. Now He would turn water into wine to keep His young friends from being shamed. That is God. That is what God is like.

So He went out and told the servants to put water in the water-pots and with a word He turned that water into wine. And so the wedding feast went on and nobody but the servants knew how narrowly that poor family had escaped being shamed before their friends. Do you think that young bride and bridegroom would ever forget the loving thing their Cousin had done for them at their marriage feast?

But how could Jesus turn water into wine? Of course He could because He was God. Will you be surprised if I say He is always doing it, that I have myself seen Him doing it dozens of times? I remember one day I was travelling through the Rhone valley in Switzerland when the thought came back to me of this miracle at the wedding. It was pouring rain. The slopes of the valley were covered with vines. The water was falling heavily on the vineyards. And I thought how in another month the vine gatherers would come and squeeze out the grapes and find that water turned into wine! That is how God gives wine to the world. That is how God gives bread to the world, when the farmer lays in God's earth his few grains of wheat and goes away to return in the autumn and find each little grain changed into 60 or 100! And stupid people don't stop to think of these wonderful miracles that God is always doing!

I don't know how Jesus turned water into wine at that wedding. And I don't know how God was doing it that day in the Rhone valley and in all the countries where I have seen Him doing it. I just bow my head in wonder at the greatness of God and delight to think that that great God is the loving Friend, as Jesus showed at that little Cana wedding.

Wine was kept in wine skins like these.

V

WHEN JESUS WAS ANGRY

NOW just a week later comes a very different story. We have been thinking of the tender kindness of Jesus about the feelings of the little bride and her friends. Now a week later we find Him fiercely angry. To understand Him aright you must see that He could be very angry at times.

Soon after that wedding He went up to Jerusalem to the Feast of the Passover, as He probably had gone every year since that time when He was a boy of twelve. There the vast crowd of Jews from every land came back every year to worship God in His holy temple. Jesus loved that house of God. He was very jealous for its honor. You remember how that boy of twelve had called it "My Father's house."

Things were going very badly now in that beautiful temple. The greedy priests and rulers had turned its lovely outer courts into a rough cattle market and were making lots of money out of the sale of cattle for the sacrifices. The shouts of the market, the rattling of money, the bleating of sheep, and the lowing of oxen disturbed even the prayers of the people in church.

The priests and rulers were growing rich. They did not care. The people were ashamed of it all, but they were afraid of the priests and could do nothing but grumble and complain. And so the people were being often cheated and the worship of God was being spoiled for the crowds who had come hundreds of miles to pray to God in His holy temple.

Young John, the disciple of Jesus who wrote our Fourth Gospel, was up in Jerusalem at this feast with Jesus, and tells us what he saw one day. The beautiful court was crowded with pilgrims waiting their turn to go into church, and all around were the trampling of cattle and the shouts of the money-changers and the buying and selling and bargaining. And the people standing by vexed and ashamed. Suddenly there is a stir at the gate and everyone turns to see Jesus, the young prophet of Galilee, marching into the court. But not the meek and lowly Jesus of our pictures, not the kindly Jesus of the Cana wedding, but a stern, masterful Jesus, striding in anger through the court like a king coming to chastise misbehaving servants. He whips the cattle out of the court, He flings down the cash desks and scatters the money on the ground. Then He turns fiercely on the priests and rulers. "Take these things hence—make not My Father's house into a cattle yard!" They try to make excuses but He will not listen to them. "Take them away! It is written in your Bible, 'My house shall be called a house of prayer,' but ye have made it a den of robbers!"

Of course the priests were terribly vexed at this. He had openly shamed them before all the people. They hated Him for it, they would never forgive Him, and two years later, at another Passover, they made their wicked plans that He should be crucified. But Jesus did not care. He was too angry to care. They had brought shame upon the holy temple of God.

Now stop and think about this anger of the Lord Jesus. Do you like it? Surely yes. You are proud and glad that He should be angry and that He should do this thing which no one else had the courage to do. It is right to think mostly of Jesus as gentle and kind and loving, but it is right to think also that He could be very angry at times. Several times He was angry at people who were mean and nasty and lying, who could hurt a little child or teach wrong things about God. So if the loving Jesus could be angry it must be right to be angry sometimes. If you saw a big bully beating a little child you ought to be angry. God would expect you to be angry then. I think He would like to see you fighting that bully.

So you see anger sometimes may be noble and good. But our anger is often neither noble nor good. Our anger is often nasty and peevish and ill-tempered. We are angry because someone has injured ourselves, or because we cannot get everything we want. Our anger is often selfish and spiteful and unforgiving. And that is all wrong and hateful and makes the world unhappy.

Now think about the anger of Jesus.

(1) He is never angry about things done to Himself. Men might reject Him, despise Him, mock at Him, spit on Him, nail Him in bitter agony on the Cross. What

did He say? "Father, forgive them, they don't know what they are doing!"

(2) His anger, too, is really part of His love. He would be fiercely angry with that bully because He could not bear to see that little child tormented.

(3) But especially remember that His anger is always on the brink of forgiveness. He may be angry with you some day if you are obstinately doing wrong and making people unhappy. But the first sign that you are sorry will touch Him into tenderness and He will take you back into His loving forgiveness again.

Now you see how grand and beautiful is the anger of Jesus. You may be angry as often as you like if you will be angry like Him. But selfish, disagreeable anger about yourself will be very disappointing to Jesus.

A money changer in Temple court.

VI

WANDERINGS IN
SPRINGTIME

I DON'T think Jesus stayed long in Jerusalem after the Passover crowds had gone home. He was not happy there. Many Jerusalem people did not like Him. So He went off to the country with some of His disciples and there, for about six months, they moved about quietly among the farmers and the village people. I think they had a lovely time. It was early summer in the country and Jesus loved the country. I think this first year was His brightest, happiest year, as He and His young comrades tramped the country roads enjoying the brown hills and the sound of running streams, talking to the children who played around the cottages, bidding pleasant good-day to the travellers whom they met. They would come on a blind man or a poor leper at a lonely crossroads and heal him. They would rest in a sunny village in the hills when they were tired.

And the country people, who knew the bitter feeling against Him in Jerusalem, would gather around in the evening, and the Master would talk to them and tell them His delightful parable stories, giving them happy thoughts of life and of God's love. And then they would be asked to someone's supper. And one day the woman of the house would have her little boy in hopeless sickness and Jesus would be told of it and lay His healing hands on the little lad and bind that mother's heart to Him for ever. I think that was how Jesus began preaching the Gospel and showing people what God was like. Not so much scolding people and frightening them about their sins, but rather helping them to see the goodness and lovableness of God. I think that is the best way to make bad people good. I think any bad people in His presence would feel sorry and ashamed and would often wish that they were a little bit like Him.

But in the midst of this pleasant time in the Judean hills He suddenly gets one day a sorrowful message. "John the Baptist has been arrested by order of King Herod and is now shut up in the black dungeon of Machaerus by the Dead Sea." And sorrow fell on Jesus and His comrades for this cruel treatment of the brave young prophet. They broke up their summer tour among the hills. And Jesus saw that the time was come that He must go forth into public life and begin openly His great life-work in the world. So I read, "Now when John was put in prison, Jesus came North to Galilee" (look in the map), "preaching the Good News of God and saying, 'The time is fulfilled, the kingdom of God is at hand, repent ye and believe the Gospel.' "

But before we follow Him to Galilee let us stay for a little to see the last of John the Baptist.

VII

HOW JOHN THE BAPTIST DIED

B EFORE following Jesus to Galilee I think you would like to delay a little while in the South to see the last of John the Baptist.

That was a horrible prison by the gloomy Dead Sea where Herod put his prisoners. Here through the long hot summer days lay the Baptist in his dungeon, accustomed all his life to the free air of heaven. Above him on the slopes was the palace of King Herod. Across the black waters lay the scenes of his boyhood and the wilderness where he had prayed and thought about the coming of Jesus. Now he is lonely and puzzled and disappointed. His great life-work is stopped. He must not preach any more about Jesus. I do not wonder that he sometimes lost heart in that horrible prison.

Sometimes his old disciples came to visit him and tell him the news. All the news that he cared for was news about his Lord. They told him of the crowds that were following Jesus and about His preaching and His miracles, I think they were a little jealous about it, for they dearly loved their brave silent master who used to have these same crowds following him until the day that he pointed away from himself to Jesus. Now they felt the dear old master is neglected and forgotten. Nobody is thinking about him now.

But John was too noble a man to think of such things. One day they talked to him about it. "It is all right," he said. "My day is over. You remember how I told you all along that I am nobody, that I am only the messenger to tell about the Christ. I am like the humble friend of the Bridegroom rejoicing in his success. I am going away into the silence, but in that silence I hear about Him. Therefore I rejoice. He must increase, I must decrease. This my joy, therefore, is fulfilled."

It takes a great and noble man to feel like that. And yet, great and noble as he was there came one day to him in that lonely prison, when he was sick and tired, a horrible fit of doubt and low spirits. He thought Jesus ought to have won the whole country to His side already. The whole nation ought to have been marching in triumph behind Him to found His Kingdom of God on the earth. Jesus seems moving so slowly. And so the awful doubt came to him for a moment and he sent two of his disciples to ask Jesus a question.

Jesus was preaching to the crowds in Galilee when He saw these two tired, sad men coming up to Him. And in a moment the whole trouble comes out. "Master, John the Baptist has sent us to ask, Are you really the Great One who should come or should we look for another?"

Ah, poor John! What an awful state of low spirits he must have got into that he should ask such a question. How horribly ashamed he would be when he thought of it afterwards. But how lovely it was to have Jesus to go to with his question. Jesus understood all about it. He always understands. He knew how that dreary prison would take the heart out of anybody. He did not much blame poor John. He sent back the men with a hopeful message and when they were gone He said to the people, "Among all men born of women there is no one greater than John."

I do hope somebody told poor John of this nice thing Jesus had said about him just when he was so lonely and so ashamed of himself for having doubted. Don't you like to think of the generous heart of Jesus, the generous heart of God who always understands us and looks for the good in us in spite of our badness?

So I think poor John was comforted even though death was coming near. One day King Herod surprised him with a visit. They got to know each other. This Herod is a queer mixture, a bad cruel man yet with some good in him. I never knew a bad man without some little good in him. Herod had not much good in him. But he liked John and listened to him, and sometimes he felt a bit sorry for his own badness. St. Mark says one of his reasons for keeping John in prison was to save him from the anger of Queen Herodias, who hated him. She was very wicked and had left her real husband to come to live with Herod. And John had openly said to the king, "You are both doing wickedly. It is not right for you to have her." Herodias was fiercely angry about that. She never forgot it and she determined some day to have her revenge on John.

Now make this picture in your minds of her revenge. It is three months later. It is King Herod's birthday and he has gathered to his birthday feast a grand assembly of his lords and captains and chief men of Galilee. The palace hall is blazing with light, and the feasting and drinking and shouting is fast and furious. In the midst of it the queen gives a special treat. She sends in her beautiful daughter Salome to dance and sing and amuse the guests. They are delighted and excited. They are half drunk already. The half-drunken king is so pleased that he swears before them all that he will give her any reward she asks for, even to the half of his kingdom.

Ah, he did not know what he was in for. The girl goes off to consult her mother and then she comes back to the shouting company. And the shouting ceases and they were horrified and sobered as that hard young voice makes its cruel demand. "You swore, O King, that you would give whatever I asked. I want you to give me in this silver dish the head of John the Baptist!"

That was Herodias' revenge on the brave Baptist! She had trapped the king into giving it. I read "the king was exceeding sorry but he was ashamed to break his promise. So he sent and beheaded John in the prison!" And the executioner brought in the bleeding head on the dish and give it to the damsel and the damsel brought it to her mother. Herod never forgot the shame and horror of it. His conscience tormented him all his days. But it was too late then. The awful thing was done.

And John's disciples took up his headless body and buried it and went and told Jesus.

That was the end of the brave, silent prophet. So he passed into the great Unseen life after death to watch again for his Lord, till two years afterwards, as we shall read later on, straight from the Cross the triumphant Christ came into that world of the Departed, and there John met again the Lord Who loved him, "the Lamb of God, Who taketh away the sins of the world."

Now you will remember that when John was put in prison Jesus went North to Galilee. In the next chapter I am trying to make you see Galilee and the lake-side where He lived for about a year and a half.

THE FOURTH BOOK

How He lived nearly two years by the Lake of Galilee teaching great truths and doing great things, and how He founded His Kingdom of God.

Keep in mind that we are now come to a new and very important time in our Lord's life, His life in Galilee, a period of about a year and a half. This is the beginning of His public teaching about God's good news to men. Here come most of the stories that we know best in the Gospels.

The Sea of Galilee where Capernaum stood.

I

A PICTURE OF GALILEE
AND THE LAKE

NOW you see where we are in our story. Jesus had decided to go North to Galilee to begin His great public teaching. (Look at the map.) Galilee is in the north, Judea is in the south. They are pretty much like Scotland and England in olden days. North was Galilee the highland province, like Scotland with its mountains and rivers and its brave highland people. South was Judea where Jerusalem was, and I don't think the people there were at all as interesting as those in the North. North and South were a bit jealous of each other.

I wish I could make you see Galilee where Jesus lived for about a year and a half and which was the scene of the stories in the Gospels that we know best. It would make things so much more interesting. Lately I have been travelling through Galilee, sailing on the Lake which Jesus knew so well and examining the ruins of the little town of Capernaum where He lived. It was very wonderful to me walking where Jesus walked, seeing what Jesus saw, and imagining in my mind Jesus moving through it all. It made the dear familiar story so much more real to me. Try if you can see it with me.

The country is not at all as bright and beautiful as it was in Jesus' day. The Turks have owned it for hundreds of years. The land was neglected. No one took care of it. The trees are cut down, the place looks desolate. So I have to think of it as Jesus saw it. Travellers of long ago have told us how it looked then. The country was well cultivated, it was thronged with bright villages. It was surrounded by rich Gentile nations who constantly travelled across it. The great white roads of the old world ran through it—the Way of the Sea that Isaiah tells of and the broad Eastern road from Arabia. And the great South Road going down to Egypt where long ago the Midianite merchants picked up Joseph on the way and sold him to Potiphar the captain of the guard, where merchant caravans with their lumbering camels, and soldiers and travellers from many lands were passing every day since the time of Abraham. Jesus could see them passing every day. Several of His parables show that He was thinking of the great white roads and the "far country" where they led to, the wicked cities where the Prodigal went.

So when you think of Jesus in Galilee, think of the mountain tribes in their gay, sunny land, of the flowers and fruits and the farmers at their work, of the men of all nations in their foreign dresses passing daily on the great white roads. Quite a busy, interesting life.

In the centre of it all you must see the Lake, the

Sea of Galilee. How I watched out for it as I came up from Nazareth one day. I had never seen it before. It seemed much smaller than I expected. A lovely little lake down in a deep valley at the base of the mountains, 680 feet below the level of the ocean. It was curious to think that around that little lake happened the central story of the world.

It seemed to me just a beautiful, lonely lake. But in Jesus' day it was not lonely. In the lands now bare of trees were pleasant woods. Where marshes are now there were lovely gardens. Where a few poor ruined little villages stand to-day was a fringe of prosperous little towns around the Lake. I saw that day but a few lonely boats on the water. In Jesus' day there were a busy fishing fleet and king's barges and a crowd of gay pleasure boats from Herod's royal town of Tiberias and the lake towns. Josephus, a great Jewish historian who lived there, tells of tropical fruits and trees of many climates bearing fruit and flowers. That is the sunny picture that belongs to the story of Jesus. That is the picture that I tried to keep in mind as I sailed on that lake with a big Jewish fisherman beside me who made me think of St. Peter pushing his clumsy oar.

Now find on the map the place where the little town of Capernaum stood on the western shore of the Lake (on the left-hand side in my picture). This is very important, for it was here that Jesus made His home in Galilee. You remember the four towns in His story. BETHLEHEM where He was born, NAZARETH where He grew up, JERUSALEM where He died, and CAPERNAUM His home by the Lake in Galilee. When I travelled last year over all that country, I was greatly interested in Capernaum by the lake-side, though the old town has been destroyed long ago and we could only find the ruins of the old houses and the pillars and parts of the synagogue where Jesus preached. But all around the country was unchanged since Jesus' day.

I stood there by the shore just where He used to sit in His little boat and teach the people crowded on the beach. I could imagine how Capernaum looked in His day. There on the slope was the Roman barrack where the good centurion lived, that heathen man whom the people praised before Jesus "for he loveth our nation and hath built us our synagogue." And that white synagogue that he built on the village street, and outside the village the rich people's homes whom Jesus knew, and down near the shore the little shops and the fishermen's houses, and the fishing boats with their rough brown sails, and the great white roads leading away into the far country. The Roman Emperor made these roads and took taxes to pay for them as travellers passed, and there where one of the white roads touched the Lake was the Roman custom house for collecting these taxes, where one Matthew whom we know sat at the receipt of taxes. Peter's house was somewhere down by the water. This would be a holy spot if I could find it, for it was in one of its little rooms that Jesus lodged whenever He was in Capernaum.

All the old familiar stories in the Gospels began to come back into my mind, and somehow they all seemed more real to me. I felt as if I could see Jesus moving about. I could see the high ground across the Lake and the country place where He went when He was tired and used to say to His disciples, Let us go across to the other side. Somewhere there on that "other side" He continued all night in prayer to God. There He found the poor lunatic wandering among the tombs. Down these slopes the herd of swine "ran violently down a steep place and were choked in the sea." There were the moors famous in Jewish history, where Sisera hurried to cool his parched throat at the tent of Jael, the wife of Heber the Kenite. There was the place where Jesus fed the five thousand people who followed Him one day when He took His tired disciples on holiday. "Come apart with Me," He said, "into the country place and rest awhile."

Try to get that whole picture clearly in your minds. The busy little fishing towns with the boats on the strand, the dark blue lake and the rough country at the farther side, and you have the picture of the central story of the Gospels when Jesus came to Capernaum.

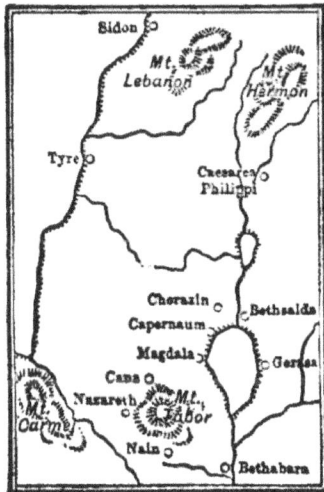

II

WHEN JESUS CAME
TO CAPERNAUM

W E are now ready for the story, How Jesus came to Capernaum. When He came up with His young disciples from the South after John was put in prison, I think they parted at the Galilee border. The young fishermen had to go home to their fishing on the Lake to wait there till He came, and Jesus seems to have wandered alone in Galilee for some weeks.

One day He came to the village of Cana. I feel sure that He went to stay with Nathaniel. You remember "Nathaniel of Cana of Galilee" who had been praying under the fig tree when he first met Jesus. And don't you think, too, that He got a delightful welcome from that little bride of Cana at whose wedding He had turned the water into wine a few months ago?

One day while He was there, there came driving post-haste into the village an officer of King Herod. Twenty miles off in Capernaum his little boy was dying. He had heard the talk in Capernaum that Jesus was coming. But that would be too late for the dying child. I can imagine the child's mother crying to him, "O don't wait. He is at Cana already. Who knows but He might come to save our boy!" Can't you see him dashing into Cana with his steaming horses? "O, Sir, my little boy is dying. Could you come and save him?" Jesus looked into his tortured face and spoke to him. But the man cannot listen. "O, Sir, come down ere my child die!" Jesus could not resist that. But He did not need to go. In a moment His thought of power went out to that sick-room in Capernaum and healed the child, and He turned quietly to the poor agonized father. "You may go home now," He said, "your child is cured."

Next morning, as his reeking horses got in sight of Capernaum, he was met by the joyful message from his wife. "When did it happen?" he asked. "Yesterday, Sir, at the seventh hour the fever left him." And the father knew that at that very hour Jesus had said to him, "Your boy is cured." And himself believed and his whole house. Don't you think Jesus would have had good friends in that officer's family when later He came to Capernaum?

A few days later Jesus followed that father on the Capernaum road. I was thinking of that story when I was there, and I felt a great desire to go over the same road following the foot-steps of Jesus. I came up from Nazareth and passed by Cana, now a poor little ruined village, and followed right on imagining Jesus before me walking on that Capernaum road. It is a rough road through the hills. Some miles on an opening in the hills suddenly shows the beautiful Lake of Galilee lying below, and the place of Chorazin and Bethsaida and Capernaum on its western shore. I thought of Jesus going down that hill road. I pictured to myself Peter and Andrew and John meeting Him on the road, and the Capernaum townspeople staring and gathering in groups as they watched their neighbors coming in with the great Stranger. And Peter taking Him to his home by the Lake and settling Him in the little room they had so lovingly prepared for Him. So I could see the whole story, How Jesus came to Capernaum.

III

PREACHING IN THE WHITE SYNAGOGUE

I HAVE told you how I came down one day by the
Capernaum road thinking of that day 2,000 years
ago when Jesus had walked that very road before
me. Then I walked by the Lake and sailed on its waters
with fishermen dressed like the disciples long ago. My
mind was still full of the stories about Jesus. In the
evening I got across to where Capernaum stood in His
day, but there were now only ruins of old houses to be
seen, and the pillars and part of the walls of the ancient
synagogue which the Roman captain built and where
Jesus preached to the people on His first Sabbath day in
Capernaum. It was curious to think of Jesus touching
these very pillars and stones which I touched and of
His voice sounding among them in the wonderful old
days.

Naturally I thought of the Bible story of the first
Sabbath when Jesus preached in this old synagogue.
Of course there would be a crowd, for the people knew
that the great Stranger was in town, and of course they
expected He would be asked to preach. I could see

in my mind the village people that morning on every path that led to the new white synagogue. Not very different, except in dress, from the people in our day in any country town going to church. The farmers and fisherfolk coming with their families. Old Zebedee the fisherman, awkward in his Sabbath clothes, with his wife and his two big sons, James and John. Andrew walking with Peter and probably Jesus walking with them. And Jairus, the ruler of the synagogue, and Herod's officer whose son had been healed, and surely with him the mother of that child to see and hear Him who had saved her boy. The village streets were thronged and bright with colors. The people were hurrying to be in time, for they expected a crowded church.

Now I see the crowded little church and I hear the prayers and the Jewish creed and Jesus joining with the others in the psalms. Then I see the ruler of the synagogue reverently bringing out the Roll of the Law and the Roll of the Prophets. This is the place for the sermon and he looks at the Stranger in Peter's seat. "Sir, we would like you to preach to the people."

So Jesus comes forward through the crowded church and begins to tell to that eager people His "good news of the Kingdom of God." We have no account of the sermon but I read, "They were astonished at His teaching, for He taught as one having authority and not as the Scribes."

But He never got that sermon finished, for in the midst it was interrupted by a poor lunatic who had got in, a man possessed with an evil spirit, and he began to shout and frighten the people, crying out, "Go away, go away, Thou Jesus of Nazareth. I know Thee who Thou art, the Holy One of God!" So Jesus had to stop and quiet the people, and then He calmly looked on the poor lunatic and with a word cast out the evil spirit and cured the man. And the people were all amazed at His mighty power. But that lunatic had stopped the sermon.

That Sabbath was a day to be remembered. Jesus walked home from church with Peter to their Sunday dinner. But the Sunday dinner was not ready. They found the housekeeper, Peter's wife's mother, suddenly taken sick with a fever and Jesus laid His hand on her and healed her.

But a more interesting thing happened in the evening. You remember one of our favorite hymns,

> "At even when the sun was set
> The sick, O Lord, around Thee lay."

It tells about this Sabbath evening. Those in Peter's house could hear hurried footsteps outside and eager talking and the sound of a gathering crowd, and when they looked out "behold the whole village was gathered together at the door." Along the waterside, among the boats and brown nets were the fevered bodies lying on their mats, and the mother with her pining baby, and a rough man leading his blind boy, and a lunatic held by strong hands. It was a sad sight for Jesus to see, but a touching, beautiful sight too. I think He just loved to see all that tender affection and sympathy of the people for their sick. God always loves to see that in people. It makes them more like to Himself.

So you can see Jesus taking up a sick baby in His arms while the sobbing mother kneels before Him and a boy on his crutches is hobbling up to Him. And the blind people are reaching out their hands. And the fevered people are eagerly waiting their turn. And His heart went out to them and He healed them all. He just loved doing that.

Surely He was tired as He lay down on His mat in Peter's room that night with the pleasant feeling that He had left so many happier and better. He wanted sleep and surely He got it, but He wanted something else more. So a great while before day Peter heard Him steal out of the house, and when he followed Him he found Him kneeling on the bare hillside resting His soul in prayer and talking to the Father in Heaven. That was His habit all His life. And He tells us to get the habit of it too if we would be strong and happy, the habit of saying our prayers to God.

St. John and St. Peter

IV

THE MAN WHO CAME
THROUGH THE ROOF

IMMEDIATELY after this famous Sabbath Jesus went away preaching through Galilee, and when He came back the people came crowding around Him. St. Mark says that immediately "it was noised abroad that He was home" (R. V. margin). You see, Capernaum is already regarded as "home."

Here comes an interesting story when another sermon of Jesus is curiously interrupted. Jesus is teaching in a crowded upper room and the people outside, who have heard that He is home, are crowded all around waiting to see Him. One could not get even near the door.

Now down the village was a poor paralyzed man on his sick-bed. There is reason to think that he had brought this sickness on himself by a sinful life. Probably he had gone away over the great white roads to a wicked heathen city, as the Prodigal son did, and there in the "far country" had ruined his health by a life of sin. Now he is miserable about his sin as well as his sickness. He thinks God could not forgive a man who had sinned so badly and probably made others sin too. And nobody, he thinks, could cure a cripple who could hardly move his limbs. So he must die and be punished by the righteous God. He is very sorry for the past but it is too late to be sorry now.

But he has a few old comrades who care for him, and one day they came to tell him of the town talk that "Jesus is home." "Jesus," they said, "has cured diseases worse than yours and Jesus is most kindly when people are most miserable. Come on, let us carry you to Him. Who knows what may happen?"

So they bring him on his stretcher. But they cannot get even near the door for the crowd. They might try again to-morrow. But to-morrow Jesus might be gone and these good fellows hated to disappoint their friend. Now that they had stirred some hope in him he longed to get near Jesus and feared to miss Him. Then a bright idea occurred to them. Sailormen have often to use their wits to get out of an awkward place. "Let us get some rope out of the boats and climb up to the roof and swing him down."

So came a curious interruption to the teaching of Jesus in that room inside. A noise in the roof, the tiles stripped away, the light shining in, and Jesus looks up to see four brown sailor faces looking eagerly down with their four cords tied in sailor knots at the corners of a mattress. And down through the roof swings the poor frightened paralytic, down to the very feet of the Lord. I can imagine His good-natured smile at the kindly trick.

"Jesus seeing their faith," says the story. He loved to see the unselfish affection for their friend, but He specially liked to see people trusting Him and determined not to be put off.

So He looked into that white face at His feet, and through the sad eyes, so wistfully calling to Him, He could see into the deep sorrow behind. Ah, Jesus knew what was troubling him most. "Cheer up, my son! Be of good cheer!" That was His favorite word to despairing people always. "Be of good cheer, thy sins are forgiven thee!"

That is how I know that the man was troubled about his sins. Jesus would never say this to him otherwise. You can see the startled wonder of the man. "Who is this that knows my inner thoughts and puts his finger right on the hidden pain?" Something in Jesus' look made him feel himself forgiven and peace came to his poor miserable heart.

But if he was surprised, everybody else was more surprised. The man had come to be healed of his disease. Why should Jesus only talk of forgiving his sins? Ah, they did not know what Jesus knew about the man's secret sorrow. And they did not feel what Jesus felt, that to cure his soul was more important than to cure his body—that to make a man a good man was more important than to make him a well man. And they did not know who Jesus was and what right He had to forgive sins.

So they were puzzled and angry and suspicious. "This man blasphemeth. Who can forgive sins but God alone!" And Jesus knew their thoughts. "You think I have not power to forgive sins." Then He turned to the poor cripple at His feet. "Arise, my son, take up thy bed and go home!" And immediately a new power came to that poor crippled man and "he arose and took up his couch and went forth before them all."

And the people were all amazed and glorified God saying, "We never saw it in this fashion."

Cannot you imagine the delight of that poor cripple and the passionate love he would feel towards Jesus? And do not you feel pretty sure that he would never forget that day when he came down through the roof, and that on all the days to come he would be a happy, faithful servant of God? That was how Jesus healed people's bodies and souls.

V

HOW JESUS CHOSE
HIS APOSTLES

JESUS, you know, had come down from Heaven to show what God is like and to tell the good news of God's fatherhood and God's kingdom. But one man could not go everywhere, and besides that in two years time He was going back to Heaven. So all the while He was looking out for a little band of faithful men whom He would train and keep close to Him and then send out with His message. These we call Apostles. Let us see how He got them.

One morning in Capernaum, after a wild, stormy night, He was out at the lakeside with a crowd around Him. A little way down were two fishing boats all battered after the night, with their nets torn and covered with sand and the poor fishermen trying to mend and clean them. They were very discouraged. They had been out all night and had caught nothing. Now four of these fishermen were already close friends of Jesus, the friends He had made that day six months ago by the Jordan. You remember how two of them, Andrew and John, had spent that wonderful evening with Him in His little lodging and learned to admire and love Him so dearly, and how they had brought to Him their brothers, Peter and James. Nobody knew and loved Him as they did.

As the people were crowding Him too closely, He called Peter to bring round his boat and then they pushed out a little from the land and He taught the people out of the boat. And then something happened. He was thinking of the discouraged fishermen who had caught nothing. He knew what that meant to poor working men.

"Now put out," He said, "into the deep water and let down your nets."

"Master," said Peter, "it seems little use. We have toiled all night and caught nothing. However, since You say it, we will let down the net."

Then in a moment they were staring in astonishment. "They enclosed a great multitude of fishes and the nets were breaking. So they beckoned to their partners in the other boat to come and help them, and they filled both the boats so that they began to sink." And great awe and wonder fell upon the men. They knew that a great miracle had happened and Peter fell down at Jesus' knees saying, "Depart from me, for I am a sinful man, O Lord!"

Of course he did not want Jesus to leave him, but he was so astonished and felt so sinful and ashamed to be in company with One so great and wonderful. But Jesus said to him, "Fear not, Peter, from henceforth thou shalt catch men instead of fishes." Then He told Peter, and Andrew his brother, and told James and John in the other boat, that He had chosen them to be His first helpers in His great mission to the world.

A few weeks later He chose another man to add to these four. And I don't think the four liked it. For this man was of a class that all good Jews hated and despised. He was one of the "publicans" or tax-gatherers. The Roman emperor, their tyrant master, ordered all Jews to pay taxes to him, and these publicans were collecting those taxes for him from their own friends, and many of them were dishonest and collected too much and kept it for themselves. So you see people would be surprised and displeased that Jesus should choose a man of that class.

But Jesus knows our hearts. He knew this man Matthew the publican was not like the rest. Matthew was surprised and pleased that Jesus was friendly with him when even his own family would not speak to him. He had never met anyone like Jesus before. Soon he grew to love Him and to wish to be a better man and to listen to His teaching near the tax office on the great white road.

I think he was always ashamed of his trade when Jesus came in to talk with him. I picture to myself one day when Jesus was in the office, a poor fisherman coming in who could not pay his taxes and that he begged Matthew to give him time to pay, not to sell his boat and nets or the cottage that sheltered his wife and child. I think Matthew wished that Jesus were not in the office that day. But he would not promise. If he were too soft with people he would never get on. And I imagine Jesus as He went out just looking at him as He looked at Peter the night of his denial—and that was all.

But after the fisherman had gone, I think somehow Matthew did not feel quite happy. And that night the thought of the fisherman's wife and child came between him and his sleep. And I do not think he sold the boat and nets next day. And I think he grew ashamed to meet Jesus and gradually began to hate his trade and to wish he could win the approval of Jesus of Nazareth.

He did not think that Jesus knew all these good thoughts of his. So you can imagine his surprise when Jesus walked into his tax office one day and said, "Matthew, I want you to follow Me and be one of My apostles!" In his surprise and delight he gave up at once all his money-making business. "He arose and left all and followed Him," who was so poor that He did not know where to lay His head. He never could forget his gratitude to Jesus for choosing him, a poor despised publican. And I think he was always ashamed of his old bad trade. He knew that partly on account of him Jesus was sneered at as "the friend of publicans." And long afterwards he wrote his "Gospel of St. Matthew," and in his list of the apostles he humbly writes down his own name as "Matthew the publican."

So now Jesus had five apostles to begin with. We do not know how He chose the others. I wish I knew the story of the day when He chose Judas Iscariot, the awful traitor who sold Him to His enemies. We shall meet him in the story later on. I wonder why Jesus ever chose him. And I wonder why Judas ever cared to be with him. I wish I knew that story.

VI

THE STORY OF TWO DINNER PARTIES

I THINK it was rather a brave thing that Matthew did when he was going away to follow Jesus. He gave a farewell dinner to the clerks in his office and to all his publican friends to say good-bye and to tell why he was going. He was not ashamed to tell his old comrades that he had become a religious man, though some of them might sneer at him for it. I don't think they did though. Especially when he told them that he had dared to ask Jesus to the dinner and that Jesus was coming! I think that greatly surprised and pleased them. Just think of it! This great man, this holy prophet coming to dine with them as friends—publicans hated and despised, whom decent Jews would not even speak to in the street!

Next day came the dinner. A wonderful dinner, with Jesus sitting as a pleasant friend with publicans and outcasts. I see Him sitting beside Matthew, dipping with him in the dish. I hear Him joining pleasantly in the talk at the table, and somehow the guests were not afraid to talk to Him. Somehow they felt that He liked them and enjoyed being with them, that, bad as they were, He saw some good in them. And all the good that was in them rose up in their hearts to meet Him, and I am sure every man at Matthew's table that day wanted to be a better man while he was there with Jesus.

Next day the priests and Pharisees heard of this dinner. They were angry and puzzled. "Why," they asked, "should a holy prophet like to be with such people?" I think it was a still stranger thing that such people should like to be with Him. The whole story of Jesus shows that publicans and outcasts liked being with Him. I read afterwards that "the publicans and sinners drew near unto Him," and that "the common people heard Him gladly." Why, do you think? Ah, because they saw that He cared for them. He made friends with them. He opened His heart to them. And all the scolding and warning in the world would not do them as much good as the feeling that He cared. Always remember that He was God. This is God's heart, God's feelings. Whenever we are asked what God is like, we can only point to Jesus. That is what God is like.

Later on came the other dinner. After one of His busy days, Jesus was invited to dine with a rich man, Simon the Pharisee. He would walk from Peter's house through the narrow streets, past the new synagogue up to the Upper Town where the rich people lived. I can see the fine dining-room and the wealthy guests and the servants in attendance. But I am not interested in them. I am thinking of a strange thing that happened. When dinner was nearly over everyone was startled by the sound of a woman crying, and there at the feet of

Jesus knelt a poor girl sobbing her heart out, "wetting His feet with her tears and wiping them with the hairs of her head."

Simon the Pharisee was very angry. He knew her as a girl in the town, a girl of bad character. How dared she intrude into his respectable house! He thought Jesus did not know about her. But Jesus did know all about her. I think of the miserable girl in the weeks before, lonely and forsaken, thinking of her sin, thinking of the innocent old home amongst the hills, and the old father and mother whom she dared not face any more, and the God whom she dare not pray to any more. No decent person would speak to her, there was no pity for her, no future, no hope here or hereafter. Until one day she had met Jesus. Perhaps she had heard Him speak of the tenderness of God seeking His lost sheep until He find it, and ventured to tell Him of her sin and her sorrow. He was gentle and kind with her. He told her of forgiveness, told her to hope.

I suppose she was thinking of all this when she crept in to Simon's feast. But Simon was angry. He could not understand. Then Jesus said to him, "Simon, let Me tell you a story. There was once a rich man who had two debtors who owed him money. One owed five hundred pence, the other owed fifty. But neither of them had money to pay. So he forgave them both. Now, Simon, which of them do you think would love him most?" "I suppose," said Simon, "the man to whom he forgave most." "You are right," said Jesus. "Now, Simon, you think that God has not much to forgive you. This poor girl thinks that her sin is so bad that God can hardly forgive her at all. So she loves much more than you do." Then He laid His hand on the poor sobbing woman at His feet. "My child, your sins are forgiven you. Go in peace."

So she went out, and I'm sure she went in peace. God had forgiven her. She would live for God in the future and all her life she would never forget what Jesus had done for her.

Two years later in this story we shall see a woman with breaking heart watching Jesus die on Calvary. Caring not for mockery or insult, she follows His dead body to the grave, and was first at that grave on the Easter morning, while it was yet dark, and saw the first sight of the risen Lord. Jesus saith unto her, "Mary!" And she fell at His feet. "My Master! My Master!" Many people believe that this was the girl who crept in to Simon the Pharisee's dinner, who is called in the Gospels Mary Magdalene.

Women at the Tomb

VII

PICTURES OF A
DAY WITH JESUS

W HAT did the Lord Jesus do every day? Of
course, different things on different days.
But you would like to watch Him for one
whole day, and St. Mark gives us the story of one of
these days. It begins in the early morning.

A lovely spring morning about March in the year
A.D. 28. He is down by the lakeside with a crowd
pressing on Him so that He has to get into a boat off
the shore and use it like a pulpit to speak to them on
the land. He sits silent for a while watching a farmer
on the hillside sowing his seed, and the crowd turns
to watch with Him.

He bids them notice that some of the seed falls on
the hard pathway and is picked up by the birds. Some
falls on thorny ground where the thorns will spring up
and choke it. Some falls on shallow ground where the
hot sun will scorch it as it grows. All that seed is lost.
But some of it falls on good rich ground where it will
bring forth good fruit.

Jesus said, That is like Me and like all preachers. We are sowing in men's hearts God's good seed, God's happy message. But some of you are not attending much and the seed is lost, as on the hard pathway. Some of you do attend, but by and by the thorns spring up, the cares and riches and amusements of life make you forget; and some are quite eager at first, but afterwards, when people dislike them or laugh at their religion, it all dies out. But for all of you who are really in earnest and receive this seed in an honest and good heart, it will bear great fruit and make you good and brave and happy children of God. That is how Jesus used to teach. Instead of preaching long sermons, He had the interesting habit of little short stories like this which would stick in people's minds.

Then He went up to Peter's house for mid-day dinner. We are not told about the afternoon, but I suppose He was out again teaching among the crowds. Now it is late evening and He is growing tired. He looked on the cool waters of the Lake. "Bring out the boat," He said, "and let us cross to the other side." I don't think Peter quite liked the look of the sky. But out they went, seven miles across in the teeth of the wind, and Jesus was so tired after His day that He fell asleep in the stern. And as He slept the spray was wetting Him and the wind was rising and the storm clouds were gathering black across the water. Soon the fierce storm broke, for this is a dangerous lake when the wind comes rushing down from the mountains. They were in serious danger. But the Master was sleeping through it all.

At last even these fishermen, accustomed to storms,

grew frightened and called to Him. Already they were learning to turn to Him in every trouble. Quietly He awoke and rebuked the winds and said unto the sea, "Peace, be still!" And the wind ceased and there was a great calm. And the men wondered and said one to another, "What manner of man is He that even the winds and the sea obey Him!"

The storm during the night had already driven the boat out of its course down to the shore where the rough Gadarene people lived. So in the dim morning light they land near an old graveyard. But scarce have they landed when they hear horrible cries among the graves and a big, murderous lunatic, stark naked, clashing his broken chains, is rushing down upon them. They know who he is, "the madman of Gadara," a man with an evil spirit in him who lived among the tombs, and no man could bind him for he broke the chains asunder, and no one had power to tame him. And always in the tombs and in the mountains, night and day, he was crying out and cutting himself with stones

Everyone feared this wild madman and would not go near the old graveyard; but Jesus had deep pity for him. He called the fierce creature to Him and with a word He cast out the evil spirit. Instantly the man grew quiet. His whole appearance changed, and the people who came up saw the Madman of Gadara sitting at the feet of Jesus, clothed and in his right mind. And with grateful heart he went about everywhere telling what Jesus had done for him, and all men wondered.

Now they are in the boat again sailing for home.

They see a big crowd watching on the Capernaum shore. News had come in about His stilling the storm. Probably some early boat had told of the Madman of Gadara. So it was an excited crowd that waited, parked so close that He can hardly get through. There is a man in that crowd struggling through to meet Him. He had been there for hours, hurrying to and fro between a sick-room and the shore. "O Master, my little daughter! She is dying! Could You come and save her?"

Probably Jesus knew the child. It did not take Him long to know children, and this poor father was Jairus, the ruler of the synagogue where Jesus used to preach on Sabbath days. So He went with him and the people crowded after Him through the narrow streets. A sick woman, who had been twelve years suffering, reached out her hand. She had not courage to speak to Him. She crept up behind Him. With a great longing in her heart she just touched His cloak and immediately she was healed! She thought Jesus did not know. But He turned at once and spoke to her and blessed her, and she went away happy and thankful.

It was only a few minutes' delay, but it seemed like an hour to the anxious father whose child was at death's door. Ah, it is too late now! There is his servant running up and whispering in his ear, "It is all over, sir. Your daughter is dead. Don't trouble the Master any more." But Jesus overheard him and saw the deep pain in the poor father's heart. "Fear not," said He. "Keep trusting Me still." So He kept on His way to the house. And you can see the tender child-love in Him as He touches affectionately the dead young face. "Talitha cumi! My little girlie, rise up!" And as the child opened her eyes He said to her mother, "Now see that something is given her to eat."

That gives you an idea of how Jesus spent His days in Capernaum. I think they were happy days for Him. Making people happy. Making people good. I think that makes a good deal of the happiness of the great God who rules all the worlds and is caring for us all.

The Pool of Siloam in Jerusalem

VIII

THE KINGDOM OF GOD

THERE was one thing above all else that the Lord Jesus wanted. There was a lovely vision always in His mind of something that He wanted to see down here on earth. He was always wishing for it and thinking of it and talking about it, trying to get people to help Him to get it. I think it was His chief reason for coming down from Heaven. It was very hard to get it, but it was always in His mind. I am sure He had been thinking of it and planning for it in His workshop in Nazareth when He was making chairs and cattle yokes in the daytime or walking on the lone hills in the evening. And now that He was out in the world as a great teacher He had always this longing in His heart.

It was the subject of His very first sermon. "The Kingdom of God is at hand." His very last teaching before He went back to Heaven was about it, "teaching the things concerning the Kingdom of God." Every time He sent out the apostles He told them, "Preach the Kingdom of God."

We have been reading of His kindly miracles and His affection for children and His pity for the sorrowful, and that people could not help loving Him and the crowds could not help following Him. But these were only little passing things. These were not the real things that brought Him down from Heaven. All the time He would be thinking of this Vision in His mind and wishing that they would help Him to get this great thing that He wanted.

What was this Vision of His that He was always talking of? He called it "the Kingdom of God" or "the Kingdom of Heaven." What did that mean? What do you think it should mean? Don't you think a Kingdom of God must surely mean a Kingdom where God was the King, where people obeyed and loved and honored God? A Kingdom of Heaven must mean something that would make earth like Heaven.

Where had He ever seen such a vision? At home in His own land in Heaven before He came. You remember how He told His disciples to pray for it and tells you to pray for it. "May Thy Kingdom come, May Thy Will be done on earth AS IT IS IN HEAVEN." As it is in Heaven. This Kingdom of God already exists up there. That was the pattern in His mind. It was not some new thing that He was planning. The picture in His mind was the memory of the glorious home that He had come from, where all were brave and good and pure and kind, living like happy children in the family of the great God and Father who loved and cared for them.

Of course He did not expect to get anything quite *as good* as Heaven down on this sinful earth, but He wanted to get as near as He could. He wanted a Kingdom like Heaven down here where people should think of God as their Father and King and try to please and love Him.

I have heard of a man who had to move from a lovely sunny land in the South to make his home in a cold far-off country. The old memories were so dear to him that he built his new house the exact pattern of the old one, and made everything as much like as he could to his memories of the happy old home vision. It reminds me of the Lord Jesus with the vision in His mind, longing to have a Kingdom of God, a Kingdom of Heaven down here with some likeness at least to the pattern in His mind.

I am trying to picture what I think was the vision in His mind of what this world would be like if everybody joined His Kingdom. This is what we would see. A bright, happy, beautiful world. Boys and girls and men and women true and generous and kindly, the sort of people that you would like to be with, the sort of people that make life pleasanter for all about them. They are just ordinary natural people, boys and girls busy with their games and amusements and lessons, men and women busy with their work, but all with the pleasant happy feeling in their hearts that they are like children in the family of the kindly Father in Heaven who is deeply interested in them.

They wake up in the morning with the sunlight on the windows and step out into God's world and say their simple little prayer. "Thanks be to Thee, O Lord. Help me not to disappoint Thee to-day." And then they go out happily to their work and their play. And Jesus sees in His vision how the whole world is happier and pleasanter because of them, how everything bad and miserable vanishes before them, all greediness and lying and bullying and spite and drunkenness and impurity, all selfishness and cruelty and poverty and misery and pain. They are such brave generous boys, such loving-hearted unselfish girls, such fine, honorable, kindly men and women, loyal to God, loyal to the Kingdom, making Jesus' lovely vision real in this world.

Dying does not frighten them at all. For dying only means stepping out of this little Kingdom of God on earth into the big real wonderful Kingdom of God in Heaven.

Don't you think this will be a very delightful world when that vision comes true? It is coming true all right. Already He has on earth a great many members of this Kingdom. You know some of them, the nice, loving, lovable people, people that you like to be with, who are trying to do what He likes and so are helping to make the world happier and better. He loves to see that. But I think He must be disappointed too because there are many still outside His Kingdom. Don't you hate to see Him disappointed? Surely you and I would not like to disappoint Him. Pray to Him, Lord, I want to be a faithful member of Thy Kingdom. May Thy Kingdom come and Thy will be done on earth as it is in Heaven.

Here is a little story that I greatly like. The Emperor Frederick the Great was visiting a village school and was questioning the children about the three great kingdoms of Nature—Animal, Vegetable and Mineral. He held up his watch. "Now what kingdom does this belong to?"

"The Mineral Kingdom."

"And this?"(holding up a flower).

"The Vegetable Kingdom."

"And now what kingdom do I belong to?"

He expected them to say, "The Animal Kingdom." But the children were puzzled. At last a little girl timidly held up her hand:

"Well, my little maid, what kingdom do I belong to?"

"The Kingdom of God, Your Majesty."

And amid solemn silence the great King bowed his head.

"Pray God that I may be worthy," he said.

IX

THE KING BEGINNING
HIS KINGDOM

NOW comes the great day when Jesus began to make His vision real, when He started His "Kingdom of God" on this earth. His visit to earth was soon to end. Next year He is to die in bitter agony on the Cross "for us men and for our salvation," and then to rise triumphant from the grave and go back into the Kingdom of God above to prepare a place for the children of His Kingdom here to go to when they die, into the big, lovely Kingdom of God in Heaven.

He could not go on much longer Himself founding His Kingdom on earth, because, you see, His visit to earth would soon be over. So, as I have told you, He decided to appoint a band of faithful men to go on with it after He was gone. He thought of choosing twelve men to begin with, who were to be His close comrades and learn to love Him and understand Him and get excited over His lovely vision. He would trust His Kingdom to them, and He told them, "You won't be alone at this task. I will be with you always to the end of the world."

That was a great day for the world when He began His Kingdom. I want you to see it.

A still summer night on the hills by the Lake of Galilee, those hills that I was looking at last year. There under the silent stars all the night long lay a solitary Man, thinking and praying, while below on the slopes and in the villages the crowds who followed Him were asleep. The Bible says, "Jesus went up into the mountain and continued all night in prayer to God." Because this was a great thing that He was going to do and He wanted help and guidance from Heaven.

Now it is dawn, with the reddening sky and the fresh breeze from the Lake and the chirping of little birds wakening to the new day. Gradually the hill slopes are dotted with people. The disciples and the multitudes are looking for Him. Suddenly He appears coming down the hill and He seems to have some great purpose on His mind. They all gather around Him. Then in the solemn wondering silence He calls twelve names. Simon! and Simon Peter comes forward. Andrew! and Andrew came. Then James and John and the others in their order, ending with Judas Iscariot, who afterwards betrayed Him.

That little ceremony on the hill that morning was one of the great events of history, the beginning of a little society, the Christian Church, which should go out through all the coming years telling of Jesus and getting people to join His lovely Kingdom of God.

Then He gave His blessing to that future Kingdom and told them what the people of that Kingdom would be like. This is called His "Sermon on the Mount." Here is just the beginning of it:—

"Blessed are the poor in spirit—the poor humble people who feel their need of God.

"Blessed are the meek—the people who are not always thinking about themselves or fighting for themselves.

"Blessed are the merciful, for they shall obtain mercy.

"Blessed are the pure in heart, for they shall see God.

"Blessed are the peacemakers, for they shall be called the children of God.

"Blessed are they that hunger and thirst after Righteousness, for they shall be filled."

That is Jesus' vision of a happy world, His Kingdom of God on earth that He bids us pray for, "Thy Kingdom come on earth as it is in Heaven." Surely earth will be growing like Heaven when His Kingdom has fully come.

So that morning Jesus started His Kingdom and sent out His apostles to teach about it and to go on teaching about it when He was gone, and then before they died they were to appoint other men to go on with it. And so it is going on still. When we go to church and say the prayers and listen to the preachers we are just going on with what the Lord Jesus started that morning by the Lake long ago.

X

THE CAPTAIN AND
HIS SERVANT

NOW watch Jesus coming down the mountain-path after His Sermon on the Mount. The new apostles are walking with Him, all excited over what has just happened. They see a poor leper with his horrible disease meeting Him on the path and reaching out his crippled hands. "O Lord, if You liked You could cure me." And Jesus said, "I will! Be thou cured!" And immediately the horrible sores were healed and the poor leper felt himself a new man. So Jesus had made another man happy, what He always loved doing. Surely the poor leper would love Him for that.

A little farther on another very interesting thing happened. They were just entering into Capernaum, where Jesus was going home to His little room in Peter's house, when they were stopped by a group of the village men with a very unusual request that He would do a kind deed for a heathen soldier. It was not often that Jews would ask favors for a heathen. But this was a very fine heathen. He was the Roman captain from the barrack on the hill, and he was greatly troubled about his young soldier servant who was dying in great pain. Of course he knew about Jesus. For months past he could not come through the village without hearing of Him and seeing the crowds around Him. One of his comrade officers was "the nobleman whose son was sick in Capernaum." You remember how he rushed off to Cana and how Jesus cured his son. I am sure this soldier friend of his knew about it and hoped that maybe Jesus would heal his poor servant too. But he was a stranger and a heathen and was afraid to ask. So these Jewish men, who admired and liked him, came to ask for him. "He is worthy," they said, "that You should do this for him, for he loveth our nation and has built us our synagogue, our white church where You have preached."

I feel quite interested in this man, for you remember how I told you that last year when I was at Capernaum I stood one day in that very synagogue and handled the stones and the broken pillars in the ruins of that old church which he had built. So now as I write this I almost feel that he is not quite a stranger to me.

So Jesus went up towards the barrack. But when the officer saw Him coming he felt that he had been too bold in asking Him to come. He sent some friends down from the barrack to say, "Lord, I am not worthy that You should come under my roof. You healed my comrade's boy when You were far away by just speaking a word. Now if You will just speak the word my servant will be healed. I believe You have power to do this."

Jesus was greatly pleased. Pleased that the man

should so greatly care for his young soldier servant, but specially pleased that this proud Roman officer, this heathen man, should believe in Him more than His own Jewish friends did. Surely Jesus must have made a great impression on him. All he had heard about Jesus, all he had learned of His power and His lovely character during those few months in that little village, made him feel that here was somebody far different from all other men, better than all other men and greater than all other men. It would make him think of the stories in his heathen religion of the old gods coming down from heaven. That was why he felt so humble before Jesus. He was only a Roman, only a heathen, but I think deep in his heart he was a better Christian than many of the people in that crowd. I think Jesus liked the man being so humble and yet so trustful. "Lord I am not worthy but I greatly want you and I trust you." So while he counted himself unworthy that Jesus should enter his house he was counted worthy that Jesus should enter his heart.

Jesus was greatly attracted by him. "Verily," He said, "I have not found so great faith, no, not in Israel." And He said to the captain, "Go thy way. As thou hast believed so be it done unto thee." And his servant was healed in that same hour.

An eastern shepherd.

XI

A BOY'S FUNERAL

T HAT was a wonderful miracle in our last chapter. But there was something next day and much more wonderful. It must have been very exciting to follow Jesus in those days. One never knew what wonderful thing might happen.

The Bible says, "The day after He went to a village called Nain and His disciples went with Him and much people." Nain was a little mountain village in South Galilee, about twenty miles from Capernaum. (Look for it in the map.) The ruins of the old village are still there and the remains of the old gateway and some ancient burial caves about a mile outside. It must have been evening, for He had already walked twenty miles.

Now Jesus and His followers are walking up the mountain-path to the village. I think it was evening for they had already walked twenty miles. Everything looked peaceful and happy till suddenly they hear in the distance a sorrowful wailing, and soon, through the village gate, came out a funeral procession. Such an awfully sad funeral! On the wicker bier the body of a dead lad bound in white grave clothes, with his head

133

and shoulders bare, and behind the bier a weeping, heart-broken woman. "He was the only son of his mother and she was a widow."

Anyone would be touched by such a sight. Jesus especially would. For His affectionate heart would feel more keenly than others. This poor woman years before had followed her husband's funeral and now here was the orphan boy that her husband had left her—her only boy. Probably he was now grown up—able to support her as Jesus Himself had supported His widowed mother when the good Joseph had died. Surely His heart was sore for this poor widow.

Respectfully He and His followers draw aside to let the widow pass with her dead son. I read He had compassion on her. But she did not notice Him. She has no thought of Him standing there on the roadside with His heart full of sympathy. I am thinking of the thousands and thousands of mothers in all the ages at the funeral of a dead son. I know that the Lord was looking down on them and that "He had compassion on them." But like this mother in Nain they never saw and never thought that He was near them, looking, thinking, caring. We have seen so many of them lately in that terrible war-time feeling like poor King David "in the chamber over the gate" when his son Absalom was dead.

We believe that Jesus is always there and "He has compassion on them." What a pity they cannot see, that they do not know. Whenever you see a funeral like that, say to yourself, "I believe Jesus is looking down and has compassion on them."

Suddenly the funeral is stopped. Jesus has stepped out from the roadside and lays His hand on the dead boy. "He touched the bier and they who carried it stood still." And then His word of power thrilled through the dead heart and brain, thrilled through that spirit world where that boy's soul had gone. "Young man, I say unto thee, Arise! And he that was dead sat up and began to speak. And Jesus delivered him to his mother." "Delivered him to his mother." It was the poor mother that He was thinking of. Don't you love to see Him do that? Wasn't it "just like Him," as we say? We reverently mean, Wasn't it just like God? Doesn't it show us what God feels? And doesn't it make us think of the lovely time that is coming when in the blessed land of the Hereafter He will take each of these boys who have died and "deliver him to his mother"? For that is what Jesus promises will be by and by.

I have heard mothers ask in the terrible war time when their boys had died in battle, "If it be true that Jesus cares and has compassion on me, why does not He raise up my boy and all our boys?" That is a hard question. What do you think? Since death means birth into a better, nobler life, I think it would be a pity to bring them back. Of course, the mother is miserable at this parting, but if she knew the wonder of the boy's new life and its exciting adventures and all the marvellous things that he is learning there in the presence of his Lord, she would never think of wishing her boy back. It would be like putting the chicken back into the egg, or like bringing the butterfly back to be a caterpillar again. I am thinking of my own dear boy who died and of the wonderful life that he is living now and the wonderful day when I shall meet him again, and I would not for all this world ask to bring him back.

Somehow I don't think Jesus liked doing it either except for some special reason. For there were many other poor mothers in Israel with dead boys as well as this poor mother in Nain, and I know that Jesus had compassion on them. But He did not bring back their boys. Only three times in His whole life did He do it, and I think He must have had some special reason. Otherwise I think He would not have done it.

So instead of bringing back their boys He teaches in His Gospel to every poor mother that her boy is in God's good care in the great, wonderful, training school above, and bids her look forward to the day when she will see him again. Her boy will be well worth waiting for when she meets him in that day when God, in His own good time, will "deliver him to his mother."

> He is not dead, the child of your affection,
> But gone into that school
> Where he no longer needs your poor protection,
>   Where Christ Himself doth rule.

XII

GOING ON HOLIDAY

W E all like holidays. We older people like them as you youngsters do, and look forward to them every year when we can get them. But we do not all think about them in the same way as we do about our work—that God likes them and is interested in them. We older people know that our work and our daily duties are God's will for us. You know that your schoolwork is God's will, sums and geography and Latin and hard lessons. He likes to see you do them well to prepare you for doing bigger things by and by.

But do we think that our holidays, when we have done our work, are also God's will for us—games and play, marbles and baseball and football and cricket and swimming and idle sailing on sunny lakes in summer? Are they God's will for us? Some people seem to think that God is only interested in our work, that holidays and enjoyment and fun are something that God just puts up with and is not interested in. Now that is all wrong. It would be bad for you to think that the things you most enjoy are something that God does not care about.

One great use of studying our Lord's life is to find out what He thinks about things. So it is very interesting to come on this story of a day when He went off with His disciples for a holiday.

He had sent them away on a difficult preaching mission through the country. Now they had just returned, dead tired from tramping the hot country roads and preaching and arguing with people who were sometimes disagreeable. They had had a hard time, and also they were troubled and vexed over the horrible news they had heard in the South, that John the Baptist had been murdered in his prison by King Herod. Now they are back, all flushed and excited and over-tired, as they tell of what they had seen and heard and done. I think the Lord was very tired too. I like to think of His being tired like one of ourselves. From morning till night the crowds were pressing round Him and His tired comrades. The Bible says they had no rest, "no leisure so much as to eat."

Then one day, when they were feeling hot and tired, Jesus spoke the very words they needed. "Let us go off for a holiday," He said. "Come away with me into a country place and rest awhile." He knew it would be good for them to get away from work and people, away amid the fields and woods and mountains, and talk and rest and enjoy themselves together.

It was a kindly thought and it shows us His thought about our holidays and rest and amusement. He likes to see us playing as well as working. He likes to see us laughing and enjoying ourselves. He likes good hearty work. But He likes, also, good hearty play after work. So Jesus teaches us that holiday time as well as lesson time, playtime as well as worktime, is something that God likes for us.

Now I see these serious grown men like a set of happy schoolboys starting off for this holiday. They are waiting on the lakeshore. Peter and another are bringing in the clumsy boat. He could not do it alone, for she was a clumsy old lugger if she was at all like what they use on the Lake to-day. Last year I sailed on that Lake in one of them, and a big fisherman, that I thought must be like St. Peter, had to stand up, stepping backward and forward at each stroke, to push the great heavy oar.

Now the Master is seated. They all clamber in. As soon as they are out in deep water, the red-brown sail is set. They are steering northeast to the country hills, away from the bustle and strain and excitement, glad to be on holiday on the sunny water, rejoicing to feel a boat under them again, laughing and talking and interrupting each other, eagerly reminding each other of their mission experiences, or sometimes, with anger and sorrow in their hearts, telling the Master what they had heard of how the brave Baptist died.

We call these men "saints." Saint Peter and Saint James and Saint John. But these "saints" as we call them to-day, as they well deserve to be called, are just ordinary natural young fishermen, such as some of ourselves know. You are not to think of solemn saintly figures with haloes round their heads, as you see in the church windows. These men in the boat are no different from other young fishermen, except that they are really religious, having a happy trust in God and a deep affection and reverence for the Master who is with them. They could enjoy seriously and happily His lovely talks with them, but they could also laugh and jest with each other, and at times tell stories of their adventures with a merry humor that must have often made Him smile in the happy gaiety of these Galilee days before the big troubles came. For "saints" need not be solemn, long-faced people. Some of the nicest and most lovable "saints" in the world to-day, though we don't call them saints, are pleasant laughing people that you like to be with, who jest with each other, who enjoy games and fun, and don't seem to worry much because deep in their hearts they are loyal to God and trust Him like little children for here and hereafter.

We do not know where this holiday party had planned to go that day or how long they meant to be away. We hope they had other holidays later. But busy people, who greatly need holidays, cannot always get them. At any rate this pleasant excursion to which they had so looked forward was interrupted and stopped on its very first day. But such wonderful things happened before that day was done that they must have felt it well worth while to have lost their holiday. Read on and you will see what stopped the holiday.

XIII

WHAT STOPPED
THE HOLIDAY

I THINK the men in the boat soon began to suspect that their holiday must be put off. As they looked back they could see a crowd gathering on the Capernaum shore looking after their boat, moving away to the opposite shore. "Let us follow Him by the Lake road," said someone, and the men in the boat saw them start off together on foot by the long rough path at the north side of the Lake, even women with sick children trying to keep up with them.

So Jesus and the disciples were hardly landed when the crowd was upon them. His plan for a quiet holiday was stopped. How pleasantly He took it! These thousands of people intruding on His resting time, spoiling His plan. But they wanted Him; wanted Him badly. That is always enough for Jesus. These mothers and sick children went to His heart. So He moved about among them, listening to their troubles, healing their sick, telling them hopeful things about the Father in Heaven. And the disciples went among them too, helping where they could.

So the long hours passed. Evening was come. And Jesus was thinking about that crowd of tired, hungry people, men and women and boys and girls so far from home. How could they ever get back over that long road without getting anything to eat? The disciples were getting uneasy about them too.

Jesus knew what He would do, but He wanted to see how far His disciples trusted His power.

"What do you think we can do, Philip?" He asked.

"We cannot do anything, Master," said Philip. "It would take two hundred shillings' worth of bread to feed them, and there are no shops out here."

By and by the other disciples came.

"Lord, send them away. Let them try to get food at some village if they can."

"No," said Jesus, "they cannot do it. We must feed them ourselves."

"Lord, it is impossible! It would take two hundred shillings' worth of bread, and there is none to be had."

"How many loaves have ye?" He asked.

"We have nothing but our own supper, just five barley loaves and a couple of fishes."

"Bring them to Me," He said. "Now bid the people sit down on the grass in rows of hundreds and fifties."

What a sight that was! Imagine about fifty rows of people sitting on the grass in their many-colored clothes, white and brown and yellow and blue, like a great garden of flower-beds, and the puzzled disciples staring at them and at each other and at the Master. "What in the world is He going to do?"

Then happened the most wonderful thing! While all eyes were fixed wonderingly on Him, I read that "Jesus took the five loaves and the two fishes, and looking up to Heaven He blessed and brake and gave to the disciples." In utter astonishment they took the loaves, and as they broke them to the people they saw the loaves got no smaller and the fishes got no less! They must have felt like men in a dream. That is the sort of thing that happens in dreams. And the hungry people ate and the children were fed and at the end there was more food left than they started with. "Gather it up to eat on the road home," said Jesus. "Let nothing be wasted." And the number of people fed was "5,000 men besides women and children." Surely a wonderful miracle.

How did Jesus make a few loaves feed that crowd? I don't know. But I know He was God and that every year He is doing things like that, making the few grains of wheat sown on the earth increase and increase till they are enough to feed the whole world.

The farmer who sows the seed does not know how this wonderful thing is done. He just spreads one bushel of wheat on the earth and then covers it up and goes away. He can do no more. Then he comes back at harvest time and finds that God has made it into fifty bushels! That is all he knows. He has got so used to it now that he does not even wonder at it. That is a pity. I think it would make him religious if he did wonder at it.

And you too. For surely it is a greater wonder even than the feeding of 5,000 men. There was once an old poet who did wonder, and it made him write in the Book of Psalms, "O that men would praise the Lord . . . for the wonders that He doeth for the children of men!"

Then Jesus dismissed the crowd and bade them go home. But they would not go. Never in all their lives had they known such a wonder as this. At first they were silent with surprise. Then they began to get excited. They cheered and shouted and hailed Him as King of the Jews. They wanted Him made King right away. You see the Galilee people did not quite understand His teaching about His "Kingdom of God." Many thought it was to be an earthly kingdom and that Jesus should reign in Jerusalem as King, like King David of old, and drive out the tyrant Romans from Israel. It was a stupid mistake, but they were ignorant people and did not understand. Jesus knew that this would make bad mischief. So He ordered the disciples to get down to the boat at once and go home, and He Himself departed up into the dark hills to wait till the crowd went away.

So the evening deepened into night and the night into midnight, and the wind was howling through the hills, and still the lonely Christ was there upon the hillside "continuing all night in prayer to God." Now the dawn is lightening in the East and He sees the disciples in their heavy boat "toiling in rowing, for the wind was against them." Suddenly in the early morning He came to them walking on the sea. They were frightened at first till they heard Him speak. "Cheer up! Be of good cheer; it is I; be not afraid!" I do love to hear Him say so often "Cheer up!"

Then all fear was gone and Peter was so ashamed of his fright that he called out, "Lord, if it be Thou, let me walk to Thee on the water." Was not it just like Peter, who often spoke without thinking, who would leap into the water first and then, when he was in, see the dangerous waves? Jesus said, "Come on," and he came, but the waves frightened him and he began to sink. "O Lord, save me," he cries. "I'm drowning!" But Jesus would not let him drown. He caught him and held him up. "Why did not you trust Me, Peter? You could have done it all right if you trusted Me."

Then He came into the boat and sailed home with these silent, wondering men. If they had been chattering and talking that morning as they sailed out, you may be sure there was no chattering or talking now. They were so full of wonder that they surely sat silent, and I think they must have felt that it was quite worth losing their holiday to see the wonders that they had seen. They had not yet quite learned that He was God, but they were learning.

XIV

A WONDERFUL WEEK

I HAVE to leave out a great many things in this part of the story. There is not room. They would make this book too big. But I must not leave out one wonderful week just before He went away from Galilee.

Away in northern Galilee, where the river Jordan rises among the mountains, is the gay little town of Cæsarea Philippi, a fashionable holiday place for rich people in summer. (Look on the map.) Out among the lone hills above the town Jesus is camping with the disciples. But they are not there for holidays. He has taken them away from people to be all alone with Himself for solemn teaching. From what you have just read, you will see that amid the crowds of people always about Him there is not time nor quiet for this. He must teach them, and there is not much time left. Though they do not know it yet, the time is coming near when He must die and leave them and they must carry on His work and His teaching and His Kingdom of God when He is gone. And they are not ready yet. They are only beginning to understand Him, only beginning to find out who He really is.

One day as they were sitting thinking on the hillside He suddenly came across to them with this question: "Tell Me, who do the people think that I am?"

"Well, Master, some like King Herod think that You are John the Baptist risen from the dead. Some say You are Elijah come back to earth. Some say that You are Jeremiah or one of the old prophets."

Then at once He sprung on them the much more important question:

"But who do ye think that I am?"

Promptly, without hesitation, Peter answered for them all,

"Thou art the Christ, the Son of the Living God!"

He was greatly pleased. His men were beginning to understand. Now they would have something worth while to teach people. Don't you see that so long as people thought of Him as only a good man all His loving deeds and His beautiful teaching would not mean so much. But when the poor sinful world should learn, This is the Son of God who has come down to us from Heaven, this affectionate Master is God and these loving deeds and beautiful teaching are just God showing His feeling towards us—don't you see what a delightful revelation this would be? No wonder Jesus was pleased. "Blessed art thou, Simon Peter! It is not men that have taught you this but My Father in Heaven!"

But He had more lessons to teach them. They would expect now that He would go out with them in power and great glory to found His Kingdom in the land. Alas! they did not know what was coming, and Jesus did not want it to catch them unprepared.

So next day came an awful shock when He began to tell them, "The Son of Man shall be delivered into the hands of men, and they shall kill Him, and the third day He shall rise again from the dead." It was a terrible surprise. They could not believe it. That Jesus should be killed! Poor Peter felt as if a cold hand had been laid upon his heart. "O God forbid!" he cried. "O Master, surely this shall not happen to Thee!"

But Jesus rebuked him. "You are thinking like men," He said, "not thinking like God. To think like men would be to save Myself from these things. To think like God means that I must not save Myself—that I must suffer everything in order to do what I came from Heaven for."

But still they could not understand. I think they only half believed it. They tried to forget it, as we all try to forget unpleasant things. And three of them at least found it easier to forget it in their astonishment at something that happened a few days later. For He had a great deal more to teach them that week. Read on and you will see.

Another view of Sea of Galilee.

XV

HOW THEY SAW JESUS IN HIS GLORY

YES, He had a great deal more to teach that week. We are not told all the things He said day after day to prepare them for teaching the world when He was gone. They had seen very wonderful things, but on the last day of that week came the surprise of their lives. They saw Jesus in His glory! They got a glimpse through the veil into that Unseen World where He belonged. For I read that after six days "He took Peter and James and John and went up into the mountain to pray and He was transfigured before them."

They were alone in the darkness of a summer night high up on the slopes of Mount Hermon. The Master was apart from them rapt in prayer. When they had said their own little prayer, I suppose the prayer that He had taught them, "Our Father who art in Heaven," they lay down to sleep in their cloaks. Some time in the night they were wakened by a feeling of brightness and glory and a sense of strange happenings. And their eyes opened on a sight never given to mortal man before!

They seemed in a new world, a world of glory. I suppose they thought they had died and gone to Heaven.

The Master was still praying. And as He prayed His whole appearance changed. His body shone with golden light, His clothes became dazzling, "exceeding white as no fuller on earth can whiten them." It seemed as if the heavens opened above them. He appeared in glory and beauty and grandeur as if He were back in the Heaven that He came from. And out of that opened Heaven came two of its great people, Moses and Elijah, who had died hundreds of years ago. They were speaking with their Master about His death and His "going out" from earth back into their world again. They spoke of His "going out" just as the others from that world, the Christmas angels, had sung of His "coming in" on the plains of Bethlehem thirty years before. It makes me think how closely their heavenly world was watching and keeping in touch with Him all the time.

The three astonished disciples stared and stared in dumb wonder till the vision seemed about to go. Then Peter could not keep quiet any longer. He felt as if He were in Heaven, and poor Peter had not been having much of Heaven lately with the hints about His Master's death, with the memory of that stern rebuke. "O Master, let us stay!" he cried. "Let us make three tabernacles, one for Thee, one for Moses, one for Elijah!" He was so astonished that he did not know what he was saying. "And while he yet spake behold a bright cloud overshadowed them and a voice came out of the golden cloud, This is My beloved Son, hear ye Him."

At this they fell on their faces and knew no more till Jesus came and touched them, and they looked up and saw only the cold dawn upon the mountain and saw no man save Jesus only. The vision was past. The gates of the Unseen World had closed again and they found they had not got to Heaven after all. But oh the wonder, the wonder of it! They could never forget it. Long afterwards St. John wrote of that night as a great reality when, as he says, "we beheld His glory, the glory as of the Only-Begotten of the Father." But Jesus bade them keep it all a secret for the present. "Don't talk of it yet," He said, "until after I have risen from the dead."

You see at once how this would raise their whole thoughts of Jesus—that He who moved about with them as a man was someone much more than a man—that He who lived with them as an affectionate comrade was worshipped and adored in Heaven?

I wonder if it taught them, too, what I think would be a delightful thing to learn, that the people who have died and gone into the great world above are still interested in our world here, interested in us, caring for us, helping us. You see, Moses and Elijah had died a long time ago and I suppose people thought they were not interested in this world any more. But here they come, knowing what Jesus is doing in the dear land that they had loved and worked for long ago, watching what is happening and going to happen, talking to Him of His death which should happen in Jerusalem next year. I am thinking, too, of the "two young men in white," who came down from that world to talk to the apostles when Jesus was ascending into Heaven. I suppose they were two young men who had died long before. Other such things, too, are told in the Bible.

I love to think that about fathers and mothers and friends who have died and gone into that world. I think of a mother who has died and gone into that world leaving her dear children. I feel sure she is remembering them and loving them still. Don't you think she may be also watching and helping and praying for them? A great many Christian people believe that and love to believe it. I myself believe it most strongly. So if your mother or anyone who greatly loved you has gone into that world, if you are doing what would please her I should advise you to keep on doing it, and if you are doing anything that would pain her I advise you to stop it right away. I think that mother love in that New Land is very dear to God, and I don't think Jesus is likely to forget what a mother in that Land says to Him about her child on earth.

I came one day lately on the story of a school cricket match which greatly interested me. The boy at the bat evidently believed that his father, who had died, could see him and was interested in him still.

A famous old cricketer had lost his sight, he was stone-blind. It was a great grief to him that he could not see his own son play the great game which he so loved. The son became the best bat of the school team and used to lead his blind father to the games. But beyond hearing the remarks of the crowd on his boy's play he got little pleasure out of it. He could see nothing of the play.

One day the old man suddenly died. The following Saturday a great school match was to be played, and the rest of the team were, of course, afraid that their best bat would be absent, but to their surprise he appeared in his flannels and said he was going to play. And he batted that day as he had never batted before. He cut and drove with courage and judgment. His companions were astonished. He rattled up a century in no time and won the match for his side. After the cheering in the pavilion had died down, a comrade said to him, "You played the greatest game of your life this afternoon." And he replied, "I couldn't help playing like that, *it was the first time my father ever saw me at the bat!*"[3]

[3]Boreham's Essays.

XVI

GOOD-BYE TO GALILEE

W E are coming to the close of the Galilee story. After the wonderful week, opening with the Great Confession and closing with the glory of the Transfiguration, Jesus seemed to His disciples in some degree changed. He seemed different, higher, greater, more apart. He is thinking more about the end. I read, "As the time drew near that He should be received up, He steadfastly set His face to go to Jerusalem." He has to go to Jerusalem to teach His gospel in the centre of the nation. He has to go to Jerusalem to die. The end is in sight.

As they go back home to Capernaum He takes them by lonely ways, by the tracks through the hills where they would be away from people. His teaching is still going on. Look at them one day as they come near home. The Master is walking in front, thinking His great thoughts, and they are straggling in twos and three behind, whispering between themselves. They do not want Him to hear. "For by the way they were disputing who should be the greatest." They knew He would not like it. Perhaps they were jealous that Peter and James and John had been chosen to be with Him that night on the mountain. Jesus did not interfere and they thought He had not noticed. But that evening as they were all resting together in Peter's house I see Him asking them with a quiet smile, "Now tell Me what you were disputing about on the road?" They look startled at each other. They see that He knows. They are ashamed and keep silent.

I see Peter's little boy rubbing against His knee. The child was fond of Him and was welcoming Him home. So He lifted him on His knee, and with the child nestling in His arms He talks to the disciples. "Look," He says, "at this child. He does not want to be the greatest. Whoever of you shall be like this little child the same will be greatest in the Kingdom of God."

So through the heart of a little child He taught them. He did not take a verse of Scripture for His text as a preacher does in church. His text was the little boy nestling in His arms, knowing that he was safe and that Jesus was fond of him, not fretting about the future or wanting to be greater than others. "I want you to become like this little child," He says.

You can understand that. Children just trust father and mother for everything. They know they are loved and cared for. That is why they are happy. Jesus wants us all to be like that, big people and little, old people and young, like happy children in the great Father's family, trusting Him and loving Him.

Jesus loved telling people that the way to be happy

is to be like a happy, trustful child, and that God likes to see that in all of us.

Why was this child happy and trustful in Jesus' arms? *Because he knew that he was loved.* He knew that Jesus was fond of him. *That is the very first lesson in religion.* Be sure that you are loved by God more than even your parents love you. To learn that is more important than even to learn that you are sinful. Nothing helps us more than to learn that we are loved and cared for. That will make us try not to be sinful. Jesus said that to be like that is to be religious; that especially pleasant in the sight of God is to have the heart of a little child.

But He had more lessons to teach from that text of Peter's little boy. He was thinking about the future, thinking of what might happen to that dear little lad as he grew up. He felt angry as He thought how that happy innocent child in His arms might be led wrong by others some day and maybe become a bad man. The very thought of it made Him angry. "It would be better," He said, "for a man to have a mill-stone tied round his neck and be cast into the sea than that he should lead one of my little ones into sin."

I don't quite know when—maybe it was next day—when He was going to leave Capernaum to go away to Jerusalem to die, that some of the Capernaum mothers came to say good-bye. They were sorry that He was going whom their children were fond of, and they wanted Him to bless the children before He went. The disciples did not want Him to be bothered with women and children just when He was so busy. "Go away," they said, "the Master cannot see you. He is too busy to be bothered with children to-day." But Jesus heard them and He was very angry. This is one of the very few times that He was angry with them. I read, "When Jesus saw it He was much displeased and said, Suffer the little children to come unto Me, and forbid them not, for of such is the Kingdom of Heaven. And He took the children up in His arms and blessed them. And He departed thence" to go up to Jerusalem to His death.

If the Lord of Heaven is like that and feels like that about children, don't you think it is rather a good thing to be alive and a good thing to come to Him with our prayers, and not a bad thing, either, to die and go to Him when the time comes.

A Rabbi

THE FIFTH BOOK

How He started on the road to Jerusalem to die, and some great things that happened on the road.

The Prodigal Son

I

HOW HE STARTED ON THE JERUSALEM ROAD

SO Jesus said good-bye to Capernaum and the Lake. "Now that the time was come that He should be received up He steadfastly set His face to go to Jerusalem." Sadly He bids good-bye to His native province which had disappointed Him at the end. As He sorrowed later over Jerusalem, so He sorrows now over these pleasant places by the Lake. He is so sorry for what they have missed. If they had only known! If they had only known! I think of Him on the Jerusalem road turning back for a last look. "Woe for thee, Chorazin! Woe for thee, Bethsaida! Woe for thee, Capernaum! If the mighty works done in you had been done long ago in Sodom it would have remained to this day."

So He faced the Jerusalem road. When I went over that road lately from Galilee to Jerusalem, I found that a man could walk it in three or four days. But I find this story of the Road up to His death is about six months long. How is that?

Well, you see, He wanted to get to Jerusalem to

tell His blessed message when the big crowds from all nations would be there at times of the Church Festivals. When He got there the great Harvest Festival was on— the Feast of Pentecost. The city was crowded. But as soon as He began to teach His enemies tried to kill Him and He had to go, because He would not let them kill Him till He had preached His message. So He taught His Good News of God outside through the country, and at the next Festival He ventured in again. And again they would not listen. They tried to stone Him and again He had to go. The third time He went in again at the Feast of Passover and taught. Then they crucified Him. He would not go out any more now. His time was come. That is why the story of the Road to His death is six months long.

Now we are to follow Him from Galilee on the Jerusalem Road the week before Harvest Festival. He sent some disciples before Him, two by two, to tell the people on the roadside towns that He was coming. One pair, James and John, were told in Samaria, "We don't want Him. We won't have Him here," and James and John were very angry. A little later, I suppose, another pair reached the village of Bethany near Jerusalem, and went to the most important house where a man called Lazarus lived with his sisters Martha and Mary. They knew about Jesus and loved all that they heard about Him and were delighted to think He would stay with them on His way when He should come. So they began to prepare for Him and when He got to Bethany He came to stay with them on His way to Jerusalem.

I don't know if they had ever seen Him before, but

this was the beginning of a very delightful friendship which was such a pleasure to the Lord in the sorrowful days to come. In this home some of His happiest days were spent. For they were real friends and Jesus had a great desire for friendship. The Bible says, "He loved Martha and Mary and Lazarus," and you can think what a pleasant thing it was when He was tired and sorrowful to have one house that He could always feel was "Home." Every time afterwards that He was near Jerusalem He seems to have stayed there. Every day in the sorrowful week before His death He went home at night to Bethany. And there He came to bid farewell to this world when He was going back to Heaven. On that day, the Bible says, He led the disciples out as far as to Bethany, and there He passed from them and was carried up into Heaven. I think surely His three Bethany friends would have been there that day, though the Bible does not tell us.

I like writing about that lovely friendship. And I like to think that Lazarus and his sisters, who made home for their Lord on earth, are with Him now to-day in His home above. "I go to prepare a place for you," He told His disciples, "that where I am there ye may be also." Don't you think there are some nice things to be looked forward to by and by when we get there?

II

HARVEST FESTIVAL
IN JERUSALEM

S O one evening about the 18th of the month Tisri,
or October, A.D. 28, I see Jesus arriving at Bethany
very tired, on His way to the Harvest Festival,
meeting these new friends, talking with Lazarus in the
garden, sitting with the sisters before He went to bed,
walking perhaps to the bend of the road from which He
could see the lights of the city where nearly a million of
Jews from many nations were assembled. To-morrow
He would go in to the Festival.

It was a gay sight that met Him next day. Jerusalem
and the whole country around is keeping holiday for
the Feast of Tabernacles, the Harvest Thanksgiving, the
brightest, gladdest holiday of all the year, the feast of a
nation resting from its work, "the feast of Ingathering
at the end of the year when thou hast gathered in thy
labors out of the field."

Everyone liked to go to this popular Festival. Multitudes are crowding the streets, men of many lands from
the Danube to the Euphrates, friends meeting friends

who had not met for a year. Thousands of people out from their houses living in the open air, dwelling in tents. Bordering every street, crowning the city walls, filling all the open spaces are the bowers of green branches of olive and vine with bunches of ripe grapes hanging over each booth. In these pleasant bowers the people kept holiday to thank God for His mercies in the past and to remind themselves of the ancient days of the nation when Moses led their fathers through the wilderness and the people dwelt in tents.

I dare say there was a good deal of careless fun and merriment without much thought of God, just as I am afraid happens sometimes at Christmas in our own day, but the chief thought of the Festival was thanksgiving to God. Hundreds of clergy were up for the services. The Temple was crowded all the day long. Amid the chanting of priests and the sounding of silver trumpets, the people rejoiced, praising the Lord. No other Festival was so joyous as this. "He who has not seen this festival," said the rabbis, "does not know what joy means."

This year the crowds have something new to talk about. Many are wondering and doubting and expecting. They are whispering about Jesus of Nazareth. They are afraid to say much for fear of the priests. Jesus has become famous this past year. Men of Galilee are disputing with men of Jerusalem, and the pilgrims from far-off lands are hearing strange things about this mysterious young prophet who some people think may be really the Great Coming One that the prophets spoke of long ago.

The priests and Pharisees and rulers of the people will not listen to such talk. They say, "He is a bad man, He is disturbing the country and upsetting the church and He ought to be put to death." But there are people in the crowds who do not believe this. They do not know what to think.

Young John the disciple is walking in the crowd listening to the talk going on around him. He remembered some of it and wrote it down afterwards in his Gospel of St. John. Listen to it.

"Where is Jesus of Nazareth? He is not here."

"What think ye? Will He not come to the Feast?"

"He is a good man."

"Nay, He is only deceiving the people."

"Think ye that He is truly Messiah the Christ?"

"Nay, how could the Christ come out of such a place as Galilee? Has not the Bible said that He is to come from Bethlehem, David's city?"

"Some think He is the Great Coming One from Heaven."

"How could He be? Why, we know where He comes from. He is only a Nazareth carpenter. When the Great One the Messiah comes He will come from the unknown. No one will know where He comes from."

Suddenly there is a hush. Jesus is passing in the crowd in His blue and white robe stained with travel, and the strangers stare eagerly to see for the first time this Man that everyone is talking about. I wonder what they felt. An English writer, Charles Lamb, once said, "I think if Shakespeare came suddenly into this room we could not help standing up; if Jesus of Nazareth came in we could not help kneeling down." I wonder did they feel like that?

By and by a crowd gathered round Him and He taught them. We are not told what He said, only that many believed in Him but some did not. I wonder why? I think if you were there, that if you were wanting to be good, there was something about Him that would win your heart at once the moment you saw and heard Him. If you were not, perhaps it might be different.

Then Jesus moved away and again John the disciple heard the talk going on:

"Is not this the Man they want to kill? And now He speaks openly and they do nothing to Him. Do ye think that our rulers know that He is the Christ?"

Ah, no! They have very different thoughts. But they dare not touch Him with that friendly crowd around. There are Jews in that crowd from far-off lands who are not a bit afraid of the Jerusalem priests, and John hears some of them say:

"When the Christ cometh can He do greater things than this Man has done?"

When the rulers heard this talk they were very angry and went off to send their police to arrest Him. So when He stood again in the crowd that evening He saw police officers watching. He knew what that meant. Sadly He turns to the people, "Only a little longer shall I be with you," He said. "Then I go My way to Him that sent Me." But the officers were good men as well as policemen, and as they looked and listened they refused to arrest Him and the rulers were very angry with them.

But St. John has more pictures in his memory. Now it is the last day, the great day of the Feast. He sees the brilliant procession to the Pool of Siloam to bring water for the great service in church. At its head are the priests in their gorgeous vestments carrying the golden pitcher, and the long procession of pilgrims in their many-colored robes, waving their branches of willow and palm, singing the songs of praise to God. Probably Jesus is in that procession. Surely He likes those praises to God.

Now they are back in church with the golden pitcher. It was a splendid sight which John the disciple saw—the crowded Temple, the grand altar with its white-robed priests, the glory of color, the waving palms, the dress of many nations, the eager faces of the worshippers. All eyes are fixed on the altar where a priest is pouring water from the golden pitcher to remind them of God giving water in the thirsty desert long ago, and of God giving blessing to people who are thirsting for Him in their hearts. At the close of this service the silver trumpets ring out and the great Hallelujah swells through the church, "O give thanks to the Lord for He is good, for His mercy endureth for ever!"

And now at the close, in the waiting silence, rings out a clear solitary voice, the voice of Jesus Himself, "if any man thirst, let him come unto Me and drink." Think of the surprise and excitement in the Temple at that moment. Was He mad that He should talk as if He were God? This strange lone prophet saying about God's gift to the thirsting souls of the world, "If any man thirst, let him come unto Me!"

At evening service they were startled again. When the golden candlesticks were lighted and the people with blazing torches sang their rejoicing for the pillar of light which had led their fathers in the desert long ago, suddenly the voice of Jesus came to them again, "I am the light of the world. He that followed Me shall not walk in darkness, but shall have the light of life."

Of course they were startled. Why, He speaks as if He were God Himself! He ought to die! And when He came out and spoke to them they took up great stones to stone Him. So He had to flee from the city and out in the villages carry on His teaching which Jerusalem would not listen to.

III

HIS THREE STORIES
ABOUT THE FATHER

W HEN Jerusalem had turned Him out and would not listen to Him, one would like to have been able to follow and listen as He taught in the villages and through the country. He taught about God's love, that God is our Father and so we ought to be like brothers to each other. He taught them about Prayer. He told how God hated sin and tried to keep us from doing it. He said that God had a work for each of us to do to try to make people happy and good, and that at the end of the world He Himself would come back to judge all men for the good and bad things they had done. He told them many other things, and some of His disciples afterwards wrote down all they could remember.

It was easier to remember because He had such an interesting way of teaching. He did not preach long sermons to people. He just got into conversation with them, or He answered questions for them, or, chiefly, He told stories which taught what He wanted. He loved telling stories. He would tell of a great King with his slaves around him in the Castle hall and little piles of money on the long red table—or of the old miser who was building new store-houses for his goods—or of a Pharisee going up into the Temple to pray—or of a rich man in his lordly mansion who neglected a poor beggar at his gate, and what happened when they both died and met each other in the spirit world after death.

There was one thing that He specially loved to teach, about God being like a Father to all of us His poor children here, and how He longs to save even the bad, disobedient ones if they would let Him.

Jesus was often teaching this, but I think St. Luke has found out for us some of the loveliest stories about it. After Jesus had died and risen and gone back to Heaven, St. Luke was writing his new book about the life of our Lord and he tried to find out if there were any things to be told that St. Matthew and St. Mark had not written. So he talked to all the old disciples that he could meet and some of them had been with Jesus on the Jerusalem road. One day he was delighted when they told him this lovely new story to put in his book. They told him that one day on the road to Jerusalem, when Jesus had come to Jericho, He had been talking and, I think, dining with a set of "publicans and sinners." Most of them were not a bit religious. But they liked Him and He liked them, though they were not very good people, and He liked telling them about God. It was just like St. Matthew's dinner in Capernaum.

Now the Pharisees and clergy and religious people

were angry that He should mix with such people, whom they would not even speak to in the street. You see, the Pharisees thought that God only cared for His good, faithful children and did not care at all for publicans and sinners and people who were doing wrong. But Jesus said, No. God cared for sinful people too and had pain in His heart for them and longed to get them back because He loved them. So He told the Pharisees three little stories, and I feel rather glad that the Pharisees were angry since they got us these lovely stories.

The first is about a farmer who had a hundred sheep and one strayed away and got lost. He was quite troubled about his poor lost sheep lest it should fall off the rocks or get eaten by wolves, so he went away through the deserts and mountains to look for it. At last he found it, and he was so glad that he carried it off on his shoulders rejoicing and said to his people, Rejoice with me, for I have found my sheep that was lost.

That is just how God feels, said Jesus, about sinners and bad people who stray away from Him. He loves them still and longs to get them back, and if He gets them there is joy in Heaven over one sinner that repenteth.

Then He told of a poor woman who had ten silver coins and lost one, and she was so anxious that she swept all the floor and searched everywhere till she found it. And then she rejoiced like the farmer with his sheep. That is just like God, He said. That is how the Father in Heaven feels about His lost children.

Maybe it was on another day that He told the story

of the father and his two sons. There was a rich farmer in his fine home. He had two sons. The younger one was very troublesome. He was a bad boy and made his father's heart sorrowful. At last he said, "I don't want my father or his home. I won't stay here at all. I'll go away to a far country and get drunk and be wicked and do what I like and have no one to stop me." His father tried to keep him but it was no use. "I won't stay here," he said. "Give me my share of your money and let me go."

So away he went along the Great White Road to one of the wicked cities in a far country, and there he did just what he liked and made friends with bad comrades and spent his money in all sorts of wickedness. But somehow he did not get much happiness out of it. Sin never makes a man happy.

And by and by, when all his money was gone, he tried to earn more to keep him from starving. But it was hard to get work till he found a man who sent him into his fields to feed pigs, and he was glad enough to get even pigs' food to eat. For months he fed pigs, miserable and ashamed, and often he thought of the happy home he had left and the father who had been so good to him. He was very sorry for what he had done. He longed to be back, but he was afraid and ashamed to face his father.

At last he could stand it no longer. One day, sitting among the pig-troughs, he made up his mind. "Whatever happens, I'll risk it. I'll go back. I would rather feed pigs for my father than here. I can never be his son any more, but maybe he would let me in as a servant. I will arise and go to my father and will say unto him, 'Father, I have sinned against heaven and before thee. I am no more worthy to be called thy son. Will you take me as one of your hired servants?' "

So he started back over that long white road. But when the old home was in sight he was afraid to go on. Then came to him the surprise of his life! The dear old father hurrying down to meet him! He had been thinking and sorrowing about him all these years and now, in his delight at getting back his boy, he ran and fell on his neck and kissed him. "O Father," cried the poor ragged tramp, "I have sinned. I am not worthy."

But the father would not listen. He saw how sorry his boy was. He forgave him right away. He hurried him to the gate. He called to the servants, "Bring forth the best robe and put it on him, put a ring on his hand and shoes on his feet, and bring hither the fatted calf to make a feast. For this my son was dead and is alive again, he was lost and is found!" And that wicked, sorrowful tramp saw the wonder of a father's love. He was forgiven for all. He was called again "My son." Do you think he would ever forget it as long as he lived?

That, said Jesus, is what the Father in Heaven feels for a sinful son who has come back to be forgiven.

That is the lovely Gospel that Jesus came to tell and this is one of His lovely ways of telling it. Are not you glad that St. Luke discovered these three little stories which Jesus had told one day on the Jerusalem Road?

IV

HOW HE BROUGHT LAZARUS BACK FROM THE DEAD

I WISH I could tell you more of these teachings of Jesus as He moved through the villages. I very much wanted to write His story of The Man with the Talents. But I have not room. You might read it for yourselves in the 25th chapter of St. Matthew.

Again, about two months later, I see Him venturing back into the city at the Feast of Dedication. I suppose He stayed the night at Bethany with Lazarus and Martha and Mary. They knew the danger before Him and I dare say they were frightened at His going into the city next morning. There the people got around Him and He taught them more about the Father in Heaven. But He startled them more than ever when He told them at the close, "I and My Father are one!"

This was an awful thing to hear. They could believe that He was a good man, a teacher and a prophet. But to claim that He was God! It made them very angry.

"Stone the blasphemer! Stone Him! Stone Him!"

The crowd went rushing for the big stones and Jesus stood alone without defense before them.

"Why do you want to stone Me?" He asked.

"Because Thou, being a man, makest Thyself God!"

It looked as if the end were come. But His time was not yet. Something of fear and wonder held them back. They must have felt something great and wonderful about Him that made them afraid. They dropped the stones, staring stupidly at Him. So Jesus walked out of the city for the last time. Next time He would let them kill Him.

So He started off again on His road, a hunted, persecuted man, sorrowful for His country and for the city that would not listen to Him. "O Jerusalem, Jerusalem!" He said, "that killest the prophets, how often would I have gathered you as a hen gathereth her chickens under her wings, and ye would not!"

Of course He would say good-bye to His Bethany friends as He passed. It was a relief to see Him safe. They hardly expected Him to come out alive. Soon He passed from them out into the wilderness again to prepare for the end. And as they said good-bye Martha and Mary little dreamed of the big sorrow that was about to fall on their happy home and how sorely they would want Jesus before they saw Him again.

A month or two later He was away with His disciples somewhere among the hills, when one day came a sudden interruption. A messenger in hot haste from the sisters in Bethany. "Lord, he whom Thou lovest is very sick." Jesus knew even as the messenger spoke that Lazarus was already dead, and He thought of the heart-broken sisters in that pleasant home. He must surely go to them. The disciples were frightened for Him. "Lord," they said, "the people there have been just trying to kill You. Must You go there again?" How greatly they feared for Him we learn from the loyal, desponding Thomas. "If He goes to Judea He goes to His death. Let us also go that we may die with Him!"

So they came to Bethany. In the beautiful springtime amid the flowers of his garden, Lazarus lay in his grave and the two sisters were breaking their hearts. Mary is weeping in her darkened room, Martha is tending her guests, the friends from Jerusalem who had come to comfort them, when suddenly somebody rushes in, "The Master is coming! He is on the road below!" And in a moment Martha is rushing to meet Him. "O, if You had been here my brother would not have died."

"Martha," He answered, "your brother shall rise again."

But that did not seem to comfort her much.

"Oh yes, Lord, I know he shall rise again at the Resurrection at the Last Day."

You see, she thought Lazarus must remain dead until the Last Day and that seemed so far away. But Jesus knew that Lazarus was living still in the spirit-world beyond the grave. His life goes on. He cannot die. "For," said Jesus, "I am the Resurrection and the Life. He that believeth on Me shall never die."

We do not know very much about that life into which Lazarus had gone away and into which some of our dear ones have gone. But we know that they are not dead nor unconscious. They are very much alive, like Moses and Elijah, who had died long ago and in that new life were so interested in what Jesus was doing on earth that they came through to talk to Him about it, as we read lately. I think it must be a very wonderful thing to die when the eyes that have closed in the darkness of death open on a light that never was on sea or land.

Martha is puzzled. She does not understand. But she leaves her puzzles with Jesus. "Well, Lord, at any rate I believe that Thou art the Christ, the Son of God, who should come into the world."

Now comes Mary to meet Him with the same cry, "Lord, if You had been here my brother would not have died." By this time the friends from Jerusalem have come out. "Show Me where you have laid him," said Jesus.

So they led Him to the garden amid the flowers of the springtime, little thinking how very soon they would be burying Jesus Himself amid the flowers of the springtime "in a garden" not far away. A great stone lay at the mouth of the tomb. Jesus said, "Take away that stone." Martha is frightened, but He silences her with a word. "Martha, did not I tell you that you shall see the glory of God?"

Now keep your eyes on the excited little crowd

around the grave and the two sisters frightened and wondering. Then Jesus raised His eyes to Heaven in thanksgiving. Then His word of almighty power went sounding into that tomb and into the great spirit-world where Lazarus had gone. "Lazarus, come forth!" Then a solemn, awful pause while the people held their breath in horror and expectation, in that pause tremendous things were happening in that borderland where both worlds meet. Then he that was dead came forth bound in the grave clothes! Jesus said, "Loose him and let him go."

Oh, can you imagine the feelings of that stupefied little crowd! What were they thinking? What were the sisters thinking? What was Lazarus thinking?

I have often wondered why Lazarus did not tell people about that new world of wonder when he had come back. Do you know what I think? That probably he had nothing to tell. Very likely after the strain and struggle of dying, there may be a brief time of repose in which nothing is known, from which one wakens refreshed as a child in the morning. Or maybe he was so dazed and puzzled with that brief sudden sight that he could hardly know at first what had happened to him.

In any case, I suppose he could not make people understand even if he did know. Just think. Could you make a blind man understand the beauty of this world, the glory of the sunset, the colors of the flowers? He does not know what color means. If you said red or green or blue or yellow he would not know what you meant. Or could you tell a stone-deaf man about lovely music? He never heard music. He would not know what you were talking about. I think we poor dull people down here are like the blind, deaf people. We could not understand the wonder of that world even if some angel told us. By and by when we come to live there we shall know. But not yet.

I think of Lazarus as a man dazed by the tremendous thing that had just flashed on him as it were for a moment. Surely he went softly all his days, a quiet silent man with a far-off look in his eyes, like one who has dreamed a wonderful dream and cannot clearly remember.

So Jesus taught again that death was not the end of life. One greater lesson was coming soon, when He Himself came back from the dead and showed us what life and death really mean.

V

HOW THEY PLANNED
TO KILL HIM

NEXT day all Jerusalem is ringing with the news. The people are wildly excited. In the shops and bazaars nothing else is talked of. Crowds are hurrying along the Bethany road to see the grave of a man who had come back from the other world. For Bethany is only a few miles away. This tremendous thing has happened at their very doors. No one could doubt it.

Of course it roused excitement and enthusiasm about Jesus. But it roused very different feelings in the Pharisees and rulers. Already they hated Him because He had publicly rebuked them and because He said He was the Son of God. Now they were positively frightened after this great miracle. They thought the whole nation might follow Him and perhaps rise in rebellion against them, and that the Roman emperor and the Roman soldiers would come and destroy everything.

That night they called a council in the house of Caiaphas the High Priest They were all angry and excited. What are we to do? This man is doing many miracles. The people are getting out of hand. If we let Him alone all men will believe on Him and the Romans will take away our place and nation."

So they argued and disputed. Some said one thing and some another. But the High Priest soon stopped that. He was a cruel man and hated Jesus. Everyone was silent as he rose in his place.

"Ye know nothing at all," he said. "There is only one way out. Don't you see that it is better that one man should die for the people that the whole nation perish not? There is only one thing to be done. This man must die!"

St. John, who tells the story, catches hold of that expression, "One man must die for the people." Ah, he says, that wicked old priest said a truth without knowing it, that the Lord Jesus must die for the people, and not for them only but for all the children of God scattered through the world.

From that hour Jesus is doomed. They sent out an order that if any man knew where He was he should tell it that they might take Him. They did not know where He was. For after the raising of Lazarus He went quietly back to the lone country places to spend the few remaining weeks with His disciples preparing for the end.

In Jerusalem the excitement was growing every day as the Feast of Passover drew near, when crowds of Jews from all nations would be gathered in the city. Everyone was asking, Will Jesus of Nazareth come? I think the rulers would rather He should not come, for if He did it might be a dangerous time, there was so much excitement about Lazarus.

But Jesus was coming. As the Passover drew near He left His retreat and set forth for Jerusalem to die. St. Mark tells this story which St. Luke had told him. "We were in the way going up to Jerusalem and Jesus went before us and we were amazed, and as we followed we were afraid. And He began to tell us what things should happen to Him."

Just shut your eyes and call up that picture in your mind. A lone mountain-path in the wild country of Ephraim, the frightened disciples with their eyes on Him who walks before them silent, apart. They are feeling all the awe and wonder about Him. They are beginning to know who He is. They feel something is about to happen. They do not know what to expect. Then He stops to tell them. "We are going up to Jerusalem, and there they will condemn Me to death, they will mock Me and spit on Me and kill Me, and the third day I shall rise again from the dead."

They were greatly afraid. Though He had warned them before, they found it hard to believe this. Surely He, who had just raised Lazarus from the dead, could not die now when all were expecting Him to do wonderful things. Yet it was all true. We know more about it now than they did then—that Jesus, the Son of God, who had come down from Heaven, must die for the sake of the poor sinful world that He had come to save.

So Jesus walked on before them with the great

thoughts in His heart. And the great spirit-world above and the angels who sang that Christmas song at His birthday watched wonderingly what men were doing to their Lord. And God in Heaven kept silence.

Another wonderful thing was happening that day though the poor frightened disciples were not thinking about it. They had enough to think about. But you might think about it.

That God and the holy angels looking on this lone Jesus going up to Jerusalem to die, could see also the whole Jewish people coming up to meet Him—without knowing it. All the Jews all over the earth were travelling up in hundreds of thousands to the Passover, "Parthians and Medes and Elamites and dwellers in Mesopotamia, in Judea and Cappadocia, in Pontus and Asia, in Phrygia and Pamphylia, in Egypt, and the parts of Libya about Cyrene, strangers from Rome, Cretes and Arabians"—all, without knowing it, coming up to meet that lonely Christ coming along the lonely Ephraim road.

Of course they could not understand any more than the disciples could. But think of the wonder of it. As these vast crowds came up to Jerusalem and were praising God for the great things He had done in the past, a black cross was raised up on Calvary and they saw, without knowing, the greatest thing ever done for them and for the world, God dying for men.

But they did not know. Alas, they did not know!

VI

THE END OF THE ROAD

THE story of the Jerusalem road is nearly over. The end of the Road is in sight. Jesus is very near Jerusalem now. In the last chapter we saw Him with His disciples moving along that lonely mountain-path. Next day that path opens into the main broad road from the North, from Galilee to Jerusalem. That road is crowded with pilgrims for the Passover. Many are from Galilee and the disciples would watch out for friends from Capernaum and go on with them talking of home news, talking chiefly about Jesus whom most people are talking about.

In such stories I love to make pictures in my mind, seeing in my mind the people and the roads and the things that are happening. You can do the same. I will show you the pictures in my mind.

First Picture. It is that same evening. I see groups of tired travellers camping for the night. In one field the Capernaum friends have got together and Jesus is with them. There in the moonlight, when the others are asleep, I see a woman draw near to Jesus. We have seen that woman before, two years ago, you remember, in a street in Capernaum walking to church with Zebedee, her husband, and her two fisher sons, James and John, to hear Jesus' first sermon in the new synagogue.

Things have changed since then. Jesus is now very famous and many people think that He will deliver Israel and found a great kingdom. She thinks that too and, like most mothers, she wants good things for her sons. So she comes to Jesus.

"Master, will You do something for me?"

"What wilt thou, mistress, that I should do for thee?"

"Grant that my two sons may sit on Thy right hand and on Thy left hand in Thy kingdom."

Ah, that poor mother! How little she knew what was coming. With kindly pity in His heart, Jesus looks on her and her two sons.

"Ye do not know what ye are asking. Are ye able to drink My cup of pain and be baptized with My baptism of suffering?"

Bravely the two sons reply, "We are able." And Jesus knew they were. He knew they would die for Him if necessary. Later on they did die for Him, both of them. Was He thinking of that when He answered:

"Ye shall indeed drink of My cup and be baptized with My baptism of sorrow, but to sit on My right hand and on My left is not Mine to give but to those whom it is prepared for."

I see that puzzled mother going back across the

fields to her rest, still wondering if her two sons would be at His right hand and His left. Think of the awful shock that was to come to her within a week, to see her Lord dying on His cross of shame and at His right hand and His left two thieves out of the jail! How could she understand that awful mystery of God's love, that Jesus of His own choice was dying on that cross for the sake of the sinful world that He had come to save?

Second Picture. Next day comes my second picture. I see the procession moving on. They are only twelve miles from Jerusalem now. That pilgrim crowd from the North is approaching. Jericho and the townspeople are crushing through the gate to see them. For the news has got abroad that Jesus, who raised Lazarus from the dead, is in that crowd. Jesus who, some people say, is the Messiah of God to deliver Israel from the Roman power. They think of Him as Zebedee's wife did.

In the crush at the gate a blind beggarman is almost trampled down.

"What does it all mean?" he asks.

"Get out of the way, man!" the people reply. "Jesus of Nazareth is passing by."

"Jesus of Nazareth!" cries the blind beggar-man all excited. "Did not He cure a blind man in Jerusalem one day?"

Suddenly a wild hope rises in his heart and his whole soul goes out in a desperate cry:

"Jesus, Thou Son of David, have mercy on me!"

The people try to silence him but nothing can silence him.

"Thou Son of David! Thou Son of David, have mercy on me!"

The shouts of the multitude are drowning his voice. But Jesus hears it, as He always hears you or me or anyone who sorely wants Him. He stopped the whole procession on the spot.

"Bring him here to Me!"

The blind man is brought and Jesus' hand is on his shoulder.

"What wilt thou, my son, that I should do unto thee?"

"Oh, Master, that I may receive my sight!"

"Receive thy sight, my son," said Jesus, and immediately he received his sight and followed Him glorifying God, and all the people when they saw it gave praise to God.

The kindly people were glad for poor blind Bartimeus. And surely Jesus was glad. He did so love doing things like that. And remember that Jesus was God. That is what God is like.

Third Picture. I am watching the procession still as it goes through the main street of Jericho under the trees. And I see the town boys climbing the trees to watch. Boys are like that always. I see a well-dressed man in the crowd straining to see over the shoulders of the crowd. But he is a small man and cannot see much. And though he is a rich man the people will not make way for him. They don't like him. For this is Zaccheus, the publican, the Chief of Customs in Jericho, who makes them pay taxes to the Roman emperor. I have told you how the Jews hated these publicans.

You remember that other publican, Matthew, in the Capernaum Customs office whom Jesus chose to be His disciple. I think this brother officer of his in Jericho knew all about that and wanted to see Matthew's friend. I think that, like Matthew, he wanted to be good and was rather ashamed of his trade, a lonely man with no good friend to talk to. He wanted to see this famous Jesus, the Great Jew who was not ashamed to make friends with publicans. So what does he do? He climbs up the trees with the boys. It may look ridiculous but he does not care.

Then came his great surprise. Jesus, as He passed, looked up into the tree and spoke to him as if He had come to Jericho specially to meet him. "Zaccheus, come down. I want to stay at your house to-day." I wonder he did not fall off the branch in his surprise. Then he learned what blind Bartimeus had learned, what you and I and all of us can learn, that no poor soul can ever long for Jesus without Jesus knowing.

So Jesus stayed with him and dined and talked with him. Don't you think Jesus knew the evil in him? Yes, surely. But He knew the good in him too. Think what it meant to that lonely man to have a friend who could understand him, and knew not only his faults but his desire to be good. Surely Zaccheus would never forget that night with Jesus. I suppose he never saw Him again on earth. Only ten days later he heard how his new Friend had been put to a shameful death in Jerusalem.

Have you any doubt that Zaccheus became His faithful follower? Do you know what he said as Jesus bade him good-bye?

"Lord, from this day forward the half of my goods I will give to the poor, and if I have wronged any man I will restore him fourfold."

That is what coming to Jesus means—not mere beliefs or pious talk, but a whole life changed to doing what Jesus would like.

That is all we know about Zaccheus. I once read somewhere an old story about him which may not be true. A very old little man every morning tending the ground around an old sycamore tree near Jericho. "Old man," said a passing stranger one day, "why do you care thus for an old sycamore tree?" "Because," said the old man, and his eyes grew young as he said it, "from the boughs of that tree I first beheld my Lord."

Now we have reached the end of the Road. The procession of pilgrims goes on from Jericho into Jerusalem.

THE SIXTH BOOK

Tells how the Lord Jesus entered Jerusalem to die. How He was crucified, dead and buried, and the third day rose from the dead and went back to His home in Heaven.

"The Sorrowful Way" a street in Jerusalem. On this path it is believed that Jesus walked to be crucified.

I

PALM SUNDAY

K EEP your eyes still on the procession of
pilgrims on the Jerusalem road with Jesus and
His disciples walking among them. They are
leaving Jericho and the shouting crowds and Zaccheus
and blind Bartimeus, who is able to see them now.

Now they are passing the village of Bethany through
rows of the Bethany people, crowded on the roadside,
to see Jesus of Nazareth who had raised their townsman
Lazarus from the dead. As He sees in the crowd the
eager faces of the Bethany family come to welcome Him,
Jesus with His disciples leaves the procession which
continues its way to Jerusalem. We leave it too, and
delay at Bethany with Jesus.

Next evening there is a supper in Bethany in His
honor and, as we should expect, "Martha served and
Lazarus was one of them that sat at meat." And Mary is in
her little room unwrapping a vase of precious ointment
to anoint the feet of the Lord. Her face is very sad, for
she knows more than others do of the secrets of Jesus,
and she fears that He is coming to Jerusalem to die. Now
she comes out with her vase of precious ointment, and

as the delightful perfume spreads through the room I am sure that many of the guests are pleased that this honor should be paid to Jesus. So they are surprised to see a man, an angry red-haired man, stand up and say it is all wrong (this was Judas Iscariot, one of the apostles, and old stories tell that he had red hair).

"Why," he asks, "should she waste this precious ointment; she should sell it and give the money to the poor and not waste it like this."

Judas is in very bad humor this night. He is a bitter, disappointed man. He had thought that Jesus would become King over Israel and that he himself would be one of His great officers, so he is disappointed and cross and would find fault with Mary or anybody.

Jesus rebuked him. "Let her alone," He said, "she is showing her love, she has done a beautiful deed, and wherever My Gospel shall be preached throughout the world this loving deed shall be told in memory of her." So you see after nineteen hundred years it is being told now to you in memory of her. If the people at that supper had known that it was the last time such a kindness should be done to Him—that within a few days He would be lying dead in Joseph's tomb—I do not think anyone there would have found fault with Mary.

The next morning is Sunday. The Bethany people awake all proud and excited. The most famous Person in the land is a guest in their village, and everyone wants to see Him who raised Lazarus from the dead, who, some people say, is the Great One from Heaven.

Their little village has become famous in a night. The whole countryside is talking of it.

I am thinking of Jesus that sunny morning, returning to breakfast from His morning prayer on the hills and the disciples coming to meet Him all excited and expecting. Surely, they think, some great thing is going to happen now. By and by, they are more excited still when Peter and John come out to tell them, "He has sent us to Bethpage to find a young ass on which never man sat. The Master is going to ride in procession to Jerusalem!"

Soon the news spread, and many began to think of the famous old prophecy in their Bible. "O daughter of Zion, behold thy King cometh, sitting on an ass's colt."

You are not to think of the ass as the common little animal of our day. The ass in those countries in the days of Jesus was often a fine animal, often used even in royal processions. I read that the Judges of Israel used to ride on white asses.

Jerusalem is only four miles away. And Jerusalem, too, is all excited. Its narrow streets are crowded with thousands of foreign Jews from all over the world, come up for the Passover. Everyone is talking of Jesus, and of Lazarus of Bethany whom He had raised from the dead, and crowds are coming out to Bethany to see the dead man who has come back from the Other World. So they meet the procession from Bethany, the Bethany people and His old friends from Galilee and the multitude who admired Him all following after the Lord. The road is lined with crowds as for a royal procession. The common road is not good enough for Him. The Galilee friends are laying down their cloaks on the road, the multitudes are spreading His path with green branches and the shouting can be heard in Jerusalem itself. "Hosanna! Hosanna to the Son of David! Blessed be the King of Israel that cometh in the Name of the Lord!"

It looks like a King of earth riding in to victory. They think Jesus should be proud and glad. But Jesus is not proud and glad. For it is not a King of earth riding in to victory. It is the King of Heaven riding in—to die.

At the top of the hill-road there is a turn to the north, and the city which had been hidden by the shoulder of the mountain bursts suddenly into view. Jerusalem! The City of God! The dream-city of the Jew! There in the sunny afternoon it lies before Him in all its beauty— with its gardens and palaces and its stately Temple of Mount Moriah with the sunlight on its pinnacles and spires and the blue cloudless sky spread out over all. No other sight could so stir the heart of a Jew.

And His heart is deeply stirred but with sorrow and pain that He could not have saved His nation and that fair city from its doom.

Oh what a glorious future might have been theirs! Here is the Lord from Heaven that their prophets have dreamed about come down to make them the centre of His Kingdom of God on earth. But they are refusing Him, they will not have Him. So they must lose that glorious future. He cannot save them. He can only die for them.

So as He looks out on that fair city before Him He utters aloud His sorrowful thought:

"Oh Jerusalem, if thou hadst only known. If thou hadst only known."

Now the procession has come to the city, and as the shouting crowd sweep in through the beautiful Golden Gate the strangers came rushing to ask what it meant, and the answer of the multitude came like a triumphant song, "This is Jesus the prophet of Nazareth of Galilee!" And the wicked priests and Pharisees cried angrily to each other, "We can never conquer Him now. Behold the whole world has gone after Him!"

I wonder what the people expected now. Did some think He would drive out Pilate and his soldiers and be King in Jerusalem with power and great armies? Ah, how little they knew!

We don't know much more about the Palm Sunday procession. By and by Jesus got away from the crowds and got where He always loved to be—in a crowd of children. Jesus entered into the Temple of God, His Father's House, where He had come twenty years before as a little boy of twelve. And lo and behold the great church was full of children, a great congregation of boys and girls come together, I suppose, for a Passover Children's Service. I fancy they had been watching the procession in the street and hearing the multitude shouting for Jesus. So now when they saw Him they shouted to welcome Him, "Hosanna to the Son of David! Hosanna to the Son of David!"[4] That is all they

[4]St. Matthew xxi. 15.

could remember of what they had been hearing outside, and Jesus, who so loves children, was pleased at their welcome. But the priests were very angry. They didn't like Jesus and were now rather afraid of Him. "Stop those children shouting," they cried, "do you hear what they are saying?"

"Yes, I hear them," He said. "Have ye never read in your Bible

> 'Out of the mouths of little children
> God is to be praised.' "

That's all we know about the Palm Sunday procession.

II

THE BEGINNING
OF THE END

T HAT was the end of Palm Sunday. On Monday
and Tuesday the Temple was crowded. Jesus
was preaching, teaching the people the Gospel
of God's Good News. The people were eagerly listening.
And the wicked priests and Pharisees were listening
too, greatly vexed that such crowds of people liked Him
and loved to hear Him. But they didn't dare to stop
Him. They were afraid of the people. That Palm Sunday
procession had frightened them.

So they tried to do Him all the harm they could.
They sent men to interrupt Him and to ask Him
dangerous questions that might get Him into trouble.
They asked Him, "Is it right that we should pay taxes
to the Roman Emperor?" That was a nasty little trap.
If Jesus said "Yes" the people would be vexed, for they
hated paying taxes. If He said "No" the Emperor would
put Him in prison.

They asked several wicked questions like that
and Jesus answered them kindly and patiently. At the

end they asked Him a question that their wise men were disputing about just then. "What is the greatest command in the Bible?" They thought He could not answer that since their wise men could not. But Jesus gave them a lovely answer. "This is the first and great commandment, Thou shalt love the Lord thy God with all thy heart. And the second is like unto it, Thou shalt love thy neighbor as thyself. These two commandments," He said, "are the whole of religion."

Surely that was a great and noble answer. The people were so pleased that the priests had to stop their questions. But they were not to get off so easily. "Wait now," said Jesus, "I am going to ask you some questions. There was once a man who had two sons and he sent them to work in his garden. The first said, I will not go, but afterwards he was sorry and went. The second said, Yes, sir, I am going, but he didn't go. Which of the two obeyed his father?"

"The first," they said.

"Yes," said Jesus, "and you are the second. God has sent you to teach these poor people and you pretend you are doing it, but you are not. You pretend to be religious and you are not. You are only doing harm to these people whom God loves."

Then as He watched their spiteful faces His anger was aroused, and the Son of God turned sternly on these proud, wicked clergy, like a King rebuking his disobedient servants. He spoke terrible words that would shame them for ever before those crowds of people.

"Woe unto you scribes and Pharisees, ye hypocrites, ye false teachers, ye blind guides, ye unfaithful servants. God sent you holy prophets and ye drove them out. God sent His own Son and you are trying to kill Him. Ye serpents, ye generation of vipers, how shall ye escape the judgment of God."

Then He turned and walked out of the Temple—and never entered it again.

How fiercely angry they were, these priests and Pharisees. They had been shamed before all the people, they would never forgive Him for this.

Now watch them that night; they have come together to the High Priest's house behind the Temple, they are full of anger and hate, they want to arrest Jesus and kill Him, but they are afraid of the people.

Was not that an awful sight, the clergymen who ought to have been teaching about the love of God now full of hate wanting to kill Jesus!

But now comes a more awful thing. The priest's servant enters the room. "Sir, there is a man at the gate wanting to come in."

"Who is he? What is he like?"

"He is a big red-headed man. He seems frightened and excited. He says he is a friend of Jesus of Nazareth."

"Bring him in at once; perhaps he will tell us where we may get hold of Jesus."

So Judas Iscariot is brought in and stands before them. "What will ye give me," he asks, "if I deliver Jesus unto you? I can find Him when He is alone and the people are not there to save Him."

So they counted out to him thirty pieces of silver and he planned with them to have their police ready to go with him to-morrow night.

That is the most awful story in the whole history of the world. A man who sold his Lord for money. A traitor who pretended to be a friend that he might betray to death the Master who loved him! No wonder the disciples said when they heard it, "The devil must have entered into him."

So Judas went back to the disciples with that horrible money in his pocket to find out how he could catch Jesus when He was alone.

III

THE FAREWELL SUPPER

T HURSDAY night. This is the night of the Jews' Passover supper. You remember how Jesus when He was a boy of twelve first went to that Passover supper twenty years ago.

It is the night before the great Passover Day when every year the Jews remembered God's great salvation of their people in Egypt long ago.

It is the night before our Good Friday when a greater salvation was to come, when the Son of God was to die on the Cross to save us all.

Jesus and the disciples are assembled at their Passover supper, His good-bye supper to them before He goes away to die. Jesus is feeling especially tender and affectionate to them this night, and surely they are feeling so towards Him. Yet we cannot help seeing that they are rather disappointing Him. He knows the loving hearts of them, but He wishes that just now they would not be disputing who was the greater and who should take the higher places at the table.

He notices another thing too. They had put off their

shoes as they came in and were sitting with hot, tired, dusty feet. At rich people's suppers there was always a slave to wash the guests' feet. But there was no slave here and no one else was humble enough to do it except the Lord of Heaven Himself who had often taught them the beauty of service. He saw that none of them had even thought of doing it. Then Jesus arose and took a basin of water, and tied a towel around Him, and began to wash the disciples' feet and wipe them with the towel. Wondering and ashamed they watched Him. When He came to Peter, Peter tried to stop Him. "Nay, Lord, You shall never wash my feet." But Jesus went on through them all. I wonder what Judas Iscariot thought as his feet were washed. Was he thinking of where those feet had carried him last night?

When all were washed Jesus sat down and rebuked them gently. "If I, your Master and Lord, have washed your feet, don't you think that you should not be too proud to wash each other's feet?" They were greatly ashamed and remembered how He used to say to them, "The greatest among you is he who serveth."

But He is not in much mood for finding fault with them just now. It is their Good-bye after their three happy years together. It is a bitter parting for them and for Him. He is feeling very tender and loving towards them. The Bible says, "Having loved His own, He loved them unto the end."

He sees His poor disciples are sorely in need of comfort. Their beloved Master is leaving them. All their beautiful hopes and plans are disappointed. They do not know what is going to happen to them. They cannot understand it at all. They are very sad. And Jesus is thinking of their sadness. Not thinking of Himself and all He has to face to-morrow. He is only thinking of them and wanting to comfort them. So after supper He talks to them.

"My children, only a little longer am I with you—but let not your hearts be troubled. Trust in God. Trust also in Me. I am going to prepare a place for you, and I will come again and receive you to Myself, that where I am there ye may be also. And don't be afraid of loneliness in the life now before you. I will not leave you orphans. I will come to you. And whatsoever ye shall ask in My name that will I do that the Father may be glorified in the Son. A new commandment I give you. As I have loved you, so must you love one another. By this shall all men know that ye are My disciples if ye have love one to another. Peace I leave with you. My peace I give unto you. Let not your heart be troubled, neither let it be afraid."

Surely it comforted them. But not very much, I think. Their sorrow was too great. But they could see how He was loving them and thinking of them and wanting to cheer them up, and surely it made them love Him more than ever. Oh, how could Judas sit and listen to this! Wouldn't you think it must surely change his wicked heart? But no. The others just noticed him slipping out into the darkness. How little they know where he is going!

Now Jesus rises to do a great solemn act that all the

world has remembered since. He wants to leave to them and to us all a remembrance of Him for ever.

The Bible says, "He took bread and blessed and brake it and gave it to them saying, 'This is My Body which is given for you. Do this in memory of Me.' After the same manner also He took the cup and blessed and gave it to them saying, 'Drink ye all of this, for this is My Blood which is shed for many for the forgiveness of sins. Do this always in memory of Me.' "

Maybe they did not quite understand just then. But all the same, all their lives after they did what He told them. And all the world over to-day Christian people keep on doing it in remembrance of Him. And we know that He is always present at that loving remembrance and that His own Divine life passes into our souls when we do it. And so through this He keeps near to us always.

This is what we call Holy Communion. Most of you are too young yet to understand or take part in it. But you have seen people in church kneeling at the Altar and taking the Holy Bread and the Holy Cup as Jesus told them. When you are old enough be sure and don't neglect to do it in loving memory of Him, and so keep closer to the dear Lord who loves you.

Now it is nearly midnight. They must go. But before they go He stands up to pray for that poor pitiful little band who will have to face the world and work and suffer for Him when He is gone. Lifting up His eyes to Heaven He prays—and surely the tears are in their eyes as they hear Him:

"Father, the hour is come. Now I am no more in the world but these are in the world, and I come to Thee. Holy Father, keep them in Thy Name. Keep them from the Evil One. Sanctify them in Thy Truth. As Thou didst send Me into the world so am I sending them. Let the world know that Thou didst send Me and lovest them as Thou lovest Me. Neither pray I for these alone but for all them that shall believe on Me through their word. Father, I will that where I am they may be with Me. O Righteous Father, the world knew Thee not, but I knew Thee and these have known that Thou hast sent Me. That the love wherewith Thou hast loved Me may be in them and I in them."

Then, when they had sung the Passover hymn,

> "O give thanks unto the Lord for He is good,
> For His mercy endureth for ever,"

they went out into the Mount of Olives.

Where it is said the Last Supper was held.

IV

IN THE GARDEN OF GETHSEMANE

THEY went out into the Mount of Olives to the Garden of Gethsemane to spend in prayer with Him the last few hours they could be together. They had to go very cautiously, for they knew the enemies were watching for Him this night. They have learned with horror that one of themselves was intending to betray Him though they did not know who that traitor was. They could hardly believe it. It was too awful.

Well, at any rate, they felt, We will be faithful. We will stand by Him. No danger or trouble could make us forsake Him. "Lord," said the poor affectionate Peter, "if all the world should forsake You I certainly will not!" How little he knew his own heart. "Ah, Peter," said the Lord, "this very night before the cock-crow you will three times deny that you know Me." No wonder that Peter should passionately reply, "If I were to die with Thee I would not deny Thee in any wise."

Likewise also said they all.

The Master in silence lets it pass. He cannot talk just

now. They are staring at Him in surprise. Some terrible secret trouble in His mind seems crushing Him down. They cannot understand it. Of course they know that pain and suffering is before Him. But they know Him too well to think that any fear of pain would trouble Him like that. They never saw anyone so crushed down. It must be some terrible secret trouble that they don't know of. He is hurrying to be alone. Alone with His Father in prayer. And yet it is touching to see the craving for some friendly hearts to be near Him in His trouble. "I must be alone," He whispers. "Keep near Me, you three. Don't be far away from Me. Tarry ye here and watch with Me."

Then under the olive trees He hurries about a stone's throw ahead of them and falls on the ground in His agony. "Oh, My Father," He cries, "if this cannot pass away, if I must go through this, Thy Will be done." And in His torment of soul, the sweat was on His Face like great drops of blood.

We cannot bear to watch Him longer. Oh, what can this terrible suffering mean? We cannot understand. But we know that He was bearing the sins of the World. The Bible says, "He was wounded for our transgressions, He was bruised for our sins. The chastisement of our peace was upon Him. With His stripes we are healed. All we like sheep have gone astray and the Lord has laid on Him the sins of us all."

Surely something like that must be the meaning of His awful suffering for us men and for our salvation. We can't talk any more about it. But we should never forget it was all for our sakes.

We don't like to read of our Lord suffering so much, but one loves to think that in all His sufferings there was such tender thought about others. I love to see Him at the supper thinking not of Himself, but about what would cheer His poor comrades. It is touching to see Him longing for their friendship in His Agony here in the Garden. And now I notice another thing that touches one greatly and makes one love Him more than ever.

Three times in His Agony He turned to His friends who were to comfort Him by keeping near Him. And they failed Him—failed Him badly every time. In the midst of His Agony He found them fast asleep! Three times He came to them and every time they were calmly sleeping as if they didn't care at all.

I know how hurt and vexed I would be if that happened to me. "Little they care about me in my troubles," I would say. Not so Jesus. He did not misunderstand them. He knew it was not that they did not care, but that they were so dead tired after the excitement of the night. Poor fellows, "their spirit is willing enough," He says, "it is only the flesh is weak." Isn't it lovely to think that this is the Jesus whom we have to turn to, who can see the good in us when all others misunderstand us?

But they have slept too long. They should have kept on guard knowing the danger around Him that night. He Himself is the first to see it coming: the flashing of lights, the sound of rough voices, the lad in the white night-robe racing to warn Him, the police creeping round through the trees "with lanterns and torches and weapons." "Wake up," He says, "behold, he that betrayed Me is here."

The frightened disciples, rubbing their sleepy eyes, see that they are surrounded. And with horror and surprise they see something else. Standing beside the officer of the police, a red-haired man, their own comrade, the friend and comrade of Jesus! "Oh, is it Judas that is betraying Him? Oh, how could he do this!"

And now the traitor comes forward into the light and they are more startled than ever as they watch his next step. In all the horrible story of Judas there is nothing more horrible than this. The policemen did not know which of the men was Jesus. So Judas gave them a sign, "The man that I shall kiss that is He. Take Him and hold Him fast." Then he came forward like a friend with his hand held out and said, "Hail, Master," and kissed Him.

Oh, how could any man do that! Surely, said the disciples, the devil must have entered into him.

Sternly Jesus looked him straight in the face. "Judas, are you betraying Me with a kiss?"

Just think of it! The man who had sat as a friend beside Him at supper. The man who had been His comrade all these three years!

Jesus had a sore enough heart without this.

But there is more to come. I am ashamed to tell you

the next thing. Jesus, to save His friends from being arrested, speaks to the officer.

"Who is it that you are seeking?"

"Jesus of Nazareth."

"I am Jesus of Nazareth. You can take Me, but let these men go, they have done nothing."

So the officer let them go. *And they went! They went!*

Don't you feel awfully ashamed of them? You wouldn't have done it, would you? They got suddenly frightened at the police in the darkness. Peter, in his excitement, slashed about with a sword and cut off a man's ear.

"Put away that sword," said Jesus. "If I wanted to escape I could pray to My Father and He would immediately send to Me legions of angels."

Then, says the Bible, "then all the disciples forsook Him and fled!"

This is where the Temple stood in Jerusalem. The picture here is not the Temple but a great church or mosque which the Mohammedans have built on the site of the Temple.

V

JUDAS AND ST. PETER

"THEN all the disciples forsook Him and fled." And Jesus was led away alone through the streets of the sleeping city with the hands of the rough Temple police on His shoulders. Through the darkness before the dawn they bring Him to the house of Annas and then to the house of Caiaphas, the High Priest, where the priests and scribes are waiting to judge Him. You remember how that High Priest had already decided "it is better that this man should die." So you see what little chance He had of a fair trial with His enemies as judges.

There is the most astonishing sight in history. The Judge of mankind at the Bar of men. The Saviour of mankind to be put to death by the men He came to save!

They call up false witnesses to tell lies about Him— that He wanted to destroy the Temple—that He has told them not to pay taxes to the Emperor. All lies. But the Prisoner stands there silent; it will be no use to deny these lies.

"Why don't you answer?" cried the angry High Priest. They are so angry that one of them struck Jesus across the face. Jesus said no angry word. You remember how He could be angry enough at times. He could be very angry if another were injured. He could be fiercely angry if one did harm to a woman or led a little child astray. But He could be grandly patient if they were ill-treating Himself.

At last the High Priest gets an answer, an answer that rather frightened him. "I swear you by the living God, tell us if you are the Christ, the Son of the Blessed One." Calmly and solemnly the answer came, "I AM, and one day ye shall see the Son of Man seated on the right hand of power and coming in the clouds of Heaven." Then the High Priest in horror rent his clothes. "You have heard His blasphemy, what is your sentence?" And they all condemned Him to be worthy of death.

And then—a horrible thing that I hate to tell. They flung the Prisoner about as only an angry Eastern mob can do, and some began to spit on Him and to blindfold Him and to play blind-man's buff with Him, crying, "Prophesy to us, Thou Christ, who is he that struck Thee?" And the officers received Him with blows of their hands.

The High Priest saw it and did not care. The councillors saw it and could do nothing, but one man, a fierce red-headed man in the crowd outside the door, saw it and it drove him mad. "Judas, when he saw that He was condemned, repented himself."

I see him rushing to the priests with wild and

haggard face. "Take back your money, take back your money! Oh, I have sinned! I have betrayed the innocent blood." I see the cold sneer of these cruel hypocrites, "What is that to us? We don't care." This makes him fiercer than ever. I see him struggling in the grasp of the Temple police, shouting fiercely at the priests, flinging his fistfuls of silver on the marble floor at their feet. Conscience has at last the wretched traitor by the throat. The horrors of hell are upon him. As the police throw him out into the street, I see him rushing away as if ridden by devils, away through the streets, through the lonely roads, away to the desolate field of the Potters.

"Oh, I kissed Him with the traitor's kiss. I thought they might not condemn Him! I thought the people might save Him! I thought He might save Himself! And I sold Him for thirty pieces of silver! I threw them at their feet but they didn't care. Nobody cares now. Except Jesus—and I have sent Him to His death. He knew I would betray Him, but He risked His life and kept me near Him. And I kissed Him with the traitor's kiss!"

Then the end, the awful end. The Bible says, "he departed and went and hanged himself." Poor wretched sinful Judas!

When Judas had been flung out, the scribes and priests went forward with the bound Prisoner in their midst. They were taking Him before the Roman Governor. For the Jews had no power to put any man to death. Only the Roman Governor can pass the death sentence. And as they pass out through the courtyard something happens that brings bitter shame and sorrow to another disciple of the Lord.

In that courtyard are a little crowd of police and servants. They had made a fire in the yard, for it was cold, and they were talking and gossiping around the fire waiting for the trial to be over. When all the disciples forsook Jesus and fled, two of them, Peter and John, began to feel ashamed and they stole back into the courtyard to see what would happen. As Peter came in the maid who kept the door looked sharply at him. "Ha! you are one of this man's disciples." The frightened Peter, startled at the question, answered suddenly with a lie, "I am not." But the girl was not satisfied. He hurried past to lose himself in the group around the fire, pretending to be at ease. But that girl would not let him alone. "Certainly you are one of them," cried several voices. "You are a Galilean. We know it by your voice." "Certainly I am not!" he answered. "I don't know what you are talking about."

Now came a worse fright. One very dangerous man, a friend of Malchus whose ear Peter had cut off.

"Did I not see you in the garden with Him?"

In the old fisher days before he knew Jesus, Peter could probably swear as well as another, and now in his fright the old habit caught him. He began to curse and to swear, "I don't even know the man."

But the curses froze on his lips. Even before he turned round he felt he had been overheard. For just at this moment Jesus was being led, bound, through the courtyard on the way to His trial. And a cock was crowing outside in the early dawn. "And the Lord turned and looked upon Peter. And Peter went out and wept bitterly."

Could Jesus ever forgive that shameful denial? Such deep sorrow as Peter's will always bring forgiveness. In the early Church they said that Peter never forgot this sin—that whenever he heard a cock crow he would get out of his bed and cry to the Lord in shame and tears. See how tenderly the Lord forgave him. Even on the Cross He was thinking of poor Peter. Think of that touching message He left with the angels at the tomb. "Go tell My disciples *and Peter*—Peter who has denied Me, Peter who is breaking his heart and thinking I have cast him out for ever. Tell him especially." Oh, no wonder Peter was so fond of Him. No wonder that burst of eager passionate devotion when he met Jesus again. "Lord, Thou knowest all things. Thou knowest that I love Thee."

So the Lord went to His death with sorrowful thoughts about His closest friends. The Twelve had forsaken Him. Peter had denied Him. And Judas—I think His keenest pain was in His thoughts about Judas.

VI

SUFFERED UNDER PONTIUS PILATE

A ROMAN court of judgment. About seven o'clock in the morning. The court is held in the open air, in the courtyard of the Governor's palace. The priests and Pharisees have brought their Prisoner here hoping to get Him condemned to death. For only a Roman court can pass the death sentence. When all is ready Pontius Pilate, the Governor, a proud, soldierly-looking man, takes his place on the judgment seat. Now we can go in and watch the trial.

This is the real trial to decide whether Jesus is to die. The priests and Pharisees are in front. Behind them a mob of rough people looking on, and on each side to keep order in the court, a row of stern-looking Roman soldiers in full uniform, with spears in hand and with the brass Roman eagles in their helmets. The Prisoner, calm and dignified, but very tired and pale after that horrible night, is standing before the judgment seat.

Pilate is looking at Him and then at the reverend scribes and priests in front. He doesn't much like these reverend gentlemen. They have given him a good deal of trouble before now, and he suspects that they have brought their Prisoner here for some spiteful purpose of their own. I think he would like to save Him if he could. At any rate he will see that He gets a fair trial. Pontius Pilate is not a bad sort of judge to have except for one thing. He has a cowardly fear of his master, that cruel old Emperor at Rome, and is afraid to do anything that might vex him.

Now he begins with the question, "What has this prisoner done?" They cry out, "He stirreth up the people. He tells them not to pay taxes to the Emperor. He says that He Himself is Christ a King."

I don't think Pilate really believes them, but he sees that this talk of being King would vex the Emperor. So he turns to ask Jesus, "Is this true? Are you a King?"— "Yes," says Jesus, "but not in the way you mean. My Kingdom is not of this world."

"Well, but what have you done?"

What had He done! How could He tell Pilate this? He had raised that dead boy to comfort his mother. He had come down from Heaven to save the world. He had taught men the tenderness of the love of God, and started a Kingdom of God on earth to make a beautiful world. But how could He tell all this to Pilate?

"Yes," He says, "I am a King, a King of all who seek the truth."

"Nonsense," says Pilate. "Who knows what is truth?"

As a heathen man he did not believe in the truth of any religion. But he sees at once that this Prisoner is just a holy, religious teacher and certainly not a rebel against the Emperor.

So he tries to get these priests to drop the charge. But they insist. "He *does* want to be a King," they said. "His own disciples say that He will set up a Kingdom. The crowds in the procession on Sunday were calling Him a King, and whoever calls himself a King is an enemy to the Emperor."

You see they want to frighten Pilate. They know he is afraid of the Emperor. And it does frighten Pilate. He fears that the Emperor might punish him severely if he should let Jesus go free. And yet he knows that is the right thing to do. What a pity that he has not the courage to do it.

Now comes a gaily dressed page boy up through the court carrying a tablet—a note from the Governor's wife. Pilate reads it.

> Have nothing to do with this just man. I have suffered many things this night in a dream because of him.
>
> CLAUDIA.

This troubles him a good deal for the Romans were great believers in dreams. He knows that an Emperor, Julius Cæsar, lost his life because he neglected a dream of his wife.

Pilate is getting uneasy. He does not know quite what to do. So when he hears that Jesus has come from Galilee he thinks of sending Him across the street to King Herod, the ruler of Galilee, who happens to be staying in Jerusalem just then. He wants Herod's opinion. Herod is pleased. He has heard so much about Jesus and would like Him to do some miracles before him. But Jesus will do no miracles for him. Jesus will not even open His lips to the cruel King who murdered John the Baptist. So Herod and his officers were very angry and mocked at Him, and put an old purple robe on Him, laughing at Him as King of the Jews, and sent Him back to Pilate.

So Pilate gets no help that way. Now he is growing nervous and losing his courage. Yet he would like to save Jesus. In a weak moment he appeals to the people. "Ye have a custom that at Passover I should set free one prisoner for you. Will ye have Jesus of Nazareth?"

"No," cries the mob with a fierce, angry shout, "not this man but Barabbas."

And the whole place rings with the cry,

"Barabbas! Barabbas! Barabbas!"

Now Barabbas was a robber.

Then Pilate utters the thought that had been troubling him all the morning. "What then shall I do with Jesus who is called Christ?"

The mob know very well what they want done with Him. The fierce cry rings out, "Let Him be crucified!" Ah, but they have not had the troubling thoughts about

Him that Pilate had. This silent Prisoner has strangely impressed him. He has talked to Him and wondered about Him. He has never seen anyone like Him before. There is a look in those Eternal eyes frightening him and yet making him think of things beautiful and high. His wife's dream, too, is troubling him.

"Crucify Him, crucify Him!"

"Why," asks Pilate, "what evil hath He done?"

But they only cry the more, "Crucify Him!"

Then Pilate gets angry.

"I will *not* crucify Him," he says, "I will scourge Him and let Him go."

So this order goes to the guard-room, and soon the white, exhausted Prisoner is strapped to the scourging-post and His blood is flowing and His nerves are quivering under the brutal lash of the executioner. Surely the lowest brutes of the Roman soldiery were in the barrack-room that morning. Who else could have the heart for horseplay with that silent tortured Man? They crush a crown of thorns upon His brow. They fling Herod's purple cloak over His bleeding shoulders. They put a reed in His right hand and mock Him crying, "Hail, King of the Jews." Pilate is outside trying to stir the people to pity for the Prisoner. Now he brings Him out before them all bound and bleeding. "Then came Jesus forth, wearing the crown of thorns and the purple robe, and Pilate said unto them, 'Behold the Man.' "

But they only received Him with howls of mockery and repeated their cry that He should be crucified.

Was ever such a moment on this earth before! The Eternal Christ of God, who had come to die for men, standing in patient dignity, bleeding and mocked, before the lowest of His creatures. Had they no heart, no pity? Had Satan entered into them too?

Pilate stands watching Him, wondering and puzzled. And now his fears come doubly back as a clear accusing voice rings out across the court:

"He ought to die because He called Himself the Son of God."

The Son of God! This frightens Pilate more than ever. He takes Jesus into his room. "Tell me," he cries, "who You really are and where do You come from?"

But Jesus gave him no answer. It is too late for answers now.

What a pity Pilate was such a coward. He cannot rouse his courage and do the right thing and set Jesus free.

So he took water and washed his hands before the people saying, "You are forcing me to do this thing. I am innocent of the blood of this Righteous Man. It is your fault."

So the poor coward, with the eyes of Jesus resting upon him, gave up the struggle. The Bible says, "Then he delivered Him unto them to be crucified."

VII

ON THE CROSS

THIS is a sorrowful, awful story, but in all its awfulness we would not miss it for anything. For it is a lovely story too of the mind of Jesus, of His patient courage, of His tender thought for others in the midst of His pain.

The soldiers have laid Him on the big black Cross. Through His hands and feet they drive the cruel spikes. Now they lift up the Cross and drop it into its socket, tearing through nerves and muscles in that cruel shock. And the Son of God in His awful pain is looking forth on the fair city that has cast Him out to die, and the soldiers throwing dice for His clothes, and the priests boasting that they have conquered Him at last, and the careless crowd out to see the sight.

But they are not all bad. There are also the sorrowful little crowd from Galilee who remember the pleasant Capernaum days, and the women of Jerusalem weeping in pity, and His friends and disciples breaking their hearts.

It is horrible to see His enemies enjoying their revenge, sneering and mocking.

"Let Him now come down from the Cross, and we will believe. He saved others, Himself He cannot save."

He hears it. He knows it. Himself He cannot save. He has come to die upon the Cross for us. If He is to save us, Himself He cannot save.

He is not even thinking of Himself but of that crowd before Him. He is so sorry for them that they should be so bad, and with sorrowful heart He turns from them to the Father in Heaven and prays:

"Father, forgive them, they know not what they do."

Think what a lovely prayer is that! He is not only forgiving them and praying for them, but His kindly heart is actually trying to find some excuse for them. "They are ignorant. They don't know who I am. They are so excited that they don't know the awful thing they are doing just now. Father, forgive them!"

Wouldn't you think that that must touch even their wicked hearts? But in the noise and shouting I think few of them heard. Only those nearest to the Cross could hear. There is some good even in the worst of us and I do believe that if they had heard that prayer some of them would have wanted to tear asunder priest and Pharisee and soldier before a hair of His blessed head were touched!

One at least did hear and it touched him to the heart. "Now there were two evil-doers crucified with Him, one on the right hand and the other at the left." Both of them at first joined in the mockery, "If Thou be the Christ, save Thyself and us." Now one of them grows suddenly silent. He holds his breath when he hears these words. Not cries of pain or curses as he would expect. "They don't know!" "Father, forgive them!" He couldn't imagine anyone saying that at such a time.

And lo! A miracle! In an instant that wicked robber is changed, suddenly converted! The beauty of Christ's character has changed him in a moment and made him feel as he never felt before, shame for his bad life, dim wishes to be good, wondering admiration for the Man who in all His pain could be pitying such people at such a time. Who can He be? They are calling Him the Christ. They are crucifying Him for calling Himself the Son of God. Who is He? What is He?

The poor robber is fainting in his pain. Death is coming near and he is frightened at dying. Maybe that brave, silent Sufferer could help him. "Jesus," he cries, "will you remember me when You come in Your Kingdom!"

And the heart of Jesus went out to the poor soul. He can scarce turn His head to look at him. His parched lips can scarcely form the words, but, like a King in His majesty, the dying Christ replies:

"Verily I say unto thee. This day shalt thou be with Me in Paradise."

So came to that poor robber forgiveness and peace. And a promise of life at the other side of death. If anyone knew, Jesus knew. If He meant anything He meant this: "To-night when our dead bodies are hanging on the Cross, you and I will be together in that great new world and we shall know each other as the two men who hung on the Cross this morning." Three hours later the Lord of that world passed in there and waited for the dying thief.

Now it is midday, twelve o'clock. Hot noon-tide. The shouting has ceased. The people are getting tired of the show and scattering over the hill. By the Cross stand the soldiers with their captain sitting his horse as still as a statue. They do not mind that a little group who had stood afar off should come near now to see their Friend die.

So "there stood by the Cross of Jesus His mother" with her friends. She doesn't care for scorn or mockery. She is the mother. No one can hold her back. There is no comfort for her now but to be near Him. She knows He is the Christ. She knows He is her Lord. But just now above all else He is her Son, the Infant who lay in her arms long ago, the bright, brave Boy of the Nazareth workshop, the Youth who worked for her when her husband died.

It is awful for her to see Him thus. And no one feels this more than He Himself. He wants to save her from seeing the worst pain coming. It is her He is thinking of. His dying eyes are looking on her and His favorite disciple John beside her. "Mother," He said, "behold thy son, who will take care of thee. My son, behold the mother that I want you to care for." And from that hour that disciple took her away to his own home.

Then came the worst part of all His suffering. The awful trouble of His soul that we couldn't understand in the Garden and we can't understand it now. We only know that the Bible says He was bearing on His heart the sins of the world. For three hours He hung there in the silence and darkness. He felt as if the Father Himself had forsaken Him. It was all for our sakes though we can't understand it. It must have been very awful when He could cry at the end of it:

"My God! My God! Why did You forsake Me!"

It was over now, and He did not feel forsaken now, but it was awful while it lasted.

Now He is near the end. His spirit is at rest. He sees a Roman soldier close to the Cross and I love to see how He believed in the kindness of that rough soldier. "I'm thirsty," He said, and the man lifted up a sponge of sour wine to His lips. I would like to have been the man that did that.

At last the end has come. He is dying. But what a lovely restful feeling it is to think, "It is over now. I have done all I came for. I have taught my poor brethren all about God's love. I am dying on the Cross for the sins of the world." So He cries aloud in the happiness of a work well done:

"It is finished. Father, into Thy hands I commend My Spirit."

And having said this Jesus died.

VIII

THE SATURDAY BEFORE EASTER DAY

S O they took His body down from the Cross that Friday night and a friend gave his own tomb in the garden to bury Him in. And then they rolled a great stone to the door of the tomb and went away—oh, so hopeless and miserable! That Saturday was a heartbreaking day for them. The beloved Master is gone, it seems for ever. They are in the depths of despair. Their hearts were bound up in Jesus. They had trusted everything to Jesus. And Jesus is dead! His enemies have conquered Him after all. "Oh, how could He have died? He who raised Lazarus from the dead. He whom we believed to be the Christ of God."

Nowhere in all the wide world that day could be found a more hopeless, despairing set of people than the disciples and friends of Jesus, who was lying cold and dead in the tomb. The spring of their life is broken. There is nothing to do now. Nothing to look forward to. Nothing to hope for. The men are miserably thinking of going back to their fishing. The sobbing women are preparing spices to anoint His dead body. Jesus is dead! The end of all things is come!

For a moment, as we think of it, our hearts are sore for them. But we know what is coming. The very next morning look at them again, dazed and astonished, wild with excitement, startled with the first hope of unutterable gladness, in the city and out of the city meeting each other, rushing to each other, crying excitedly to each other, "The Lord is risen! He is come back from the dead! He has appeared to Peter! He has spoken to Mary! He has sent messages to us all. We are to meet Him in Galilee!"

At first "they believed not for joy." It was too good to be true. Can't you imagine the delight of that Easter morning to them!

I am bringing you now to hear one of themselves tell about it all long after to the boys and girls of Ephesus.

IX

HOW THE BOYS AND GIRLS OF EPHESUS HEARD ABOUT EASTER

I WISH I had been present on the day that Jesus rose from the dead. And that you knew little or nothing about it. Then the story would be so much more exciting for both of us.

Whenever you are told the story of the Lord's Resurrection, you have to hear it from someone who only learned it out of the Bible. A story of 1,900 years ago.

The boys and girls of Ephesus learned it in a much more delightful way. They with their parents were told it by a man who had been there at the time, who had seen with his own eyes the wonderful thing that had happened.

This was the dear old Bishop of their Church whom everyone was so fond of. The Sunday before he died he got up into the pulpit and because he was too sick to preach he just stretched out his hands affectionately over them and said:

"My little children, love one another. This is what my dear Lord taught me to tell you, and it is enough."

Then they took him back to his bed to die. I don't think they could easily forget that sermon.

Do you know who this old Bishop was?

You remember young John the disciple who so loved Jesus, to whom Jesus on the Cross gave His mother to take care of. This was that same John who was now a very old man, and he was always thinking about his dear Lord. His thoughts were ever turning back to the past to those three wonderful years, when he had walked the fields of Galilee with Jesus. "The disciple whom Jesus loved." Those years seem much more wonderful now that he knew who Jesus really was, the Lord from Heaven.

He was lonely now. All the old comrades were gone. James and Peter and Andrew and all of them were long ago departed to be with their Master in that other big World, and he was left alone with his precious memories of the past.

> "I'm growing very old. This weary head
> That has so often leaned on Jesus' breast
> Is bent and hoary with its weight of years.
> I'm old, so old I cannot recollect
> The faces that I meet in daily life,
> But that dear Face and every word He spake
> Grows still more clear as others fade away."

And how the people loved to hear the old man's

memories of those years. One day he was telling them of his hopeless sorrow and misery when he saw Jesus dead, and then he tells of the first little dawning of hope. Something had suddenly happened that set his heart bounding with delight. "Then I saw and believed," he says.

"Master, tell us. What did you see? Why did you believe?"

"I will tell you. It was this way. On the first day of the week Mary Magdalene went early to the tomb while it was yet dark. She saw the stone rolled away and the tomb empty. She was terrified and rushed back to tell Peter and me. We ran full speed to see. I was younger than Peter and could run faster. So I got there first and I looked into the tomb and I saw it was as Mary had said, but I did not go in. Then Peter arrived and went straight in and I saw him staring very hard at the empty grave clothes. Then I went in, and when I saw all that Peter had seen, then I saw and believed."

Thus the old man told of the first startled dawning of hope. But I can imagine his people asking, "Is that all?"

"All! Why, no. I am only speaking of my first hope that the Lord was risen. After that we saw Him—over and over again. Sometimes I was present. Sometimes I was not."

"But, Master, tell us of what you remember of that time yourself."

"I remember that day after Peter and I got back.

We were eagerly trying to tell what we had seen when suddenly Mary Magdalene burst in on us again all trembling and excited. 'Oh, I have seen the Lord! Actually seen Him! He has spoken to me! He bade me come and tell you. I didn't know Him at first. I was frightened at the empty tomb and I thought He was the gardener who might tell me what had happened. He just looked at me for a moment and my heart stood still! And then—He just called my name in the old familiar tones, "Mary!" And I knew! I knew! I fell down at His feet and cried, "Oh, my Master! my Master!" And He bade me come and tell you all.'

"That evening we were again all together. We had fastened the doors for fear of the Jews. We were talking and wondering and half afraid to hope yet. We had only seen just an empty tomb. Some of the women had told us of angels at the tomb. But we did not believe them. We were half afraid even to believe Mary Magdalene. But Peter had just come in with a strange new look in his eyes, and he told us positively and solemnly that the Lord had appeared to him. He would not talk about it. He has never talked about it since. We were greatly excited. Two disciples from the Emmaus road had also just come in and were eagerly trying to get a chance to speak. But they couldn't get a chance for the cries of delight that met them. 'The Lord is risen!' 'The Lord is risen!' 'He has appeared to Peter!' When at last they did get the chance they told us a wonderful story. How Jesus had met them and walked and talked with them on the Emmaus road and 'was known unto them in the breaking of bread.'

"So we listened and wondered and hoped and rejoiced. Then—suddenly—a solemn silence fell—JESUS WAS PRESENT! No one had heard Him come. No one had unbarred the door. But He was there! We were frightened. We thought it was a ghost. But He looked on us in the old way and spoke in His own voice. We heard His old familiar greeting, 'Peace be unto you,' and we could doubt no longer. It was no ghost. It was Himself in radiant bodily form! And, oh, we disciples were glad when we saw the Lord!

"Thomas was away somewhere. I remember how we told Thomas that night and he would not believe us. 'It is impossible,' he said. 'You must be mistaken. Unless I shall see the wounds and the print of the nails, I will not believe.'

"All that week we went about dazed like men in a dream. The following Sunday the Lord came to us again. We never knew when He would come or from whence. This time Thomas was with us. And I shall never forget how He talked to Thomas and showed him His wounded hands and side, and how Thomas was so astonished and so broken with joy that he could only fall down and worship and cry, 'My Lord and my God!' "

"But Master, you saw Him at other times too?"

"Oh yes, we saw Him many other times during the Forty Days after the Resurrection. I must tell you especially of one of these days. We had been told by the Lord to meet Him in Galilee. So we were back in the old homeland, back in Capernaum at the lakeside with all its memories of the old happy days together. One morning as we waited a wonderful thing happened. We had been out all night fishing in Peter's boat—Peter and my brother James and I and Thomas and Nathaniel and two others. We had no success. All night we had toiled and rowed and flung the nets, but we caught nothing, just as on that other day three years before when He first called us. Just at dawn we saw Him on the shore. Oh, I knew, I felt sure it was He, but I could not speak. The others did not know Him in the dim morning light.

"Then we heard a voice clearly across the water. 'My children, cast your nets on the right side of the boat and ye shall find.' They cast the net wearily and without much hope. But the moment they tried to pull it in a great wonder and dread fell on them. They couldn't pull it in it was so heavy with fishes. Just what happened that other day three years ago.

"Then I couldn't keep quiet any longer. 'Oh,' I cried, 'it is the Lord! It is the Lord!' And Peter threw himself straight into the water, for we were near the land, and we all got into the little boat and hurried after him. And there was Jesus Himself on the shore! Jesus my Lord and my God!

"Then when we had breakfasted on the fish the Lord asked Peter, 'Simon, son of Jonas, lovest thou Me?' 'Indeed I do, Lord.' 'Then feed My lambs.' And again He asked, 'Simon, do you really love Me?' 'Oh Lord, You know I do.' And then He asked the third time and I saw that Peter was hurt that He asked the third time, but he cried, 'Lord, You know all things. You know that

I love You.' Then He told how Peter would one day lay down his life for Him.

"I was just behind. Peter turned and looked at me. They used to call me 'the disciple whom Jesus loved,' and Peter asked:

"'Lord, what shall John do?'

"How I waited for the answer.

"I don't know yet what it meant.

"'If I will that he lives till I come back, what is that to thee?'

"'Dear Master, could it have meant that you are not to die at all?'

"'Ah, I know not. I have lived so long now and the rest have all died long ago. And that saying did go forth among the disciples at the time that I might not die. Yet I know that He didn't say that but "If I will that he stay till I come back." ' "

That was how the old bishop told them about the Resurrection and that was how the story got written in the Gospel of St. John, the Gospel of an old man's memories.

X

HOW THE LORD WENT BACK HOME TO HEAVEN

FOR forty days after the Resurrection the disciples lived all excited in a new world of wonder and romance and delight that the beloved Master was back with them again. He had not disappointed them after all. He had conquered death and come back victorious to be their Friend and Master for ever.

But there is a great change in their positions. It is no longer as in the old days when He lived as a man with men, as a comrade among comrades. It is a very different life—a higher and more wonderful and mysterious life that the Lord is living now. They feel that He is someone far above them, someone who seems belonging to another world. He appears among them for awhile and then vanishes away. When doors are shut and barred, He comes into the midst of them. He comes, but no one sees Him coming. He tells them to meet Him in Galilee but does not go with them. When they are there He is suddenly beside them.

He does not eat food or live in a house with them.

He does not need such things now. He used to be often hungry and thirsty. He was sometimes tired and glad of rest and shelter in the Bethany home. All this is changed. The risen Lord needs no rest or shelter. Forty days He remained on earth but in no earthly home. They see He is living a wonderful, mysterious life like what they used to read about angels in the Bible.

And so a feeling of awe and wonder comes on them. They feel that they cannot be free and familiar with Him as in the old days. They used to be like brothers going about together. One of them used to lean on His breast at supper. All this is over. We read now of their worshipping Him and bowing before Him as My Lord and My God.

So came to them more fully the great lesson that it is the Lord from Heaven that had been their Comrade and Friend, and that He can be near them even when they do not see Him.

But though He was different they felt He was just the same to His friends as ever. The same affectionate friendship was around them still. His love was, as in the old days, strong and unchanged. In all the deep feelings of His heart towards them He was just the same Jesus.

He taught them many things in this wonderful forty days. He taught them much about His Kingdom of God that He wanted on earth, that band of loyal hearts who would follow Him for love of Him—the true men and loving women and brave, loyal boys and girls that should live on this earth making it good and beautiful and then step off the edge of the world when they died into the lovely adventure of the Kingdom of God in Heaven.

Then He told them that His visit to earth was over, that He must now go back to His eternal throne in Heaven. "I came forth from the Father," He said, "and came into the world, and now I leave the world and go back to the Father." But you are not to be frightened or lonesome at My going, for I shall be looking down always and watching over you. "Lo, I will be with you always, even unto the end of the world." You can come to Me and tell Me all your thoughts and I will always hear, and God will be round you all the time.

That was why they were not troubled about His going back to Heaven. You might think they would be very sad parting with Him again, but the Bible says that after they had parted from Him *They returned to Jerusalem with great joy.* So you see how they trusted Him and believed what He said.

So one day came their last meeting, the final farewell. He was teaching His last lesson "of the things concerning the Kingdom of God." "All power is given unto Me in Heaven and in earth. Go ye therefore and make disciples of all nations, baptizing them in the Name of the Father and of the Son and of the Holy Ghost. Teaching them to do all things whatsoever I have commanded you. And, lo, I am with you always, to the end of the world."

Then He led them out to Bethany for the final Good-bye. And He lifted up His hands in blessing. And while

He blessed them He was parted from them and carried up into Heaven. Jesus of Nazareth was gone!

Surely there was joy in Heaven when their Lord went back home.

I am thinking of the day at the beginning of this story when He came down for His great adventure on the earth and the angels were crowding over the ramparts of Heaven, singing, "Glory to God in the Highest and on earth peace. For unto you is born this day in the city of David a Saviour who is Christ the Lord!"

And I am thinking of this day at the close of our story when He returned to the Father with His great adventure accomplished, carrying the thoughts of us on His heart for ever, and I am imagining again the crowded ramparts of Heaven, crowded in joyous welcome to their victorious Lord. "Lift up your heads, O ye gates, and be ye lifted up, ye everlasting doors, and the King of Glory shall come in. Who is the King of Glory? Even the Lord of Hosts, He is the King of Glory."

The Golden Gate—Jerusalem

GOOD-BYE

NOW, boys and girls, good-bye. We have finished with our story. But have we finished with the Life of Christ?

Surely not! Only just thirty years of it. Only just a chapter in the middle of it. Only just the story of His visit to earth.

All the rest has to be written yet. All the unspeakable wonders of the ages before He came to us when He was planning those countless worlds that we see floating in the sky. All the wonderful things He has done for us since He went back that day. And all the wonderful things still before Him in the future till everything bad and wrong is done away. Till Death and Hell, the Evil and the Evil One shall be swept out of God's great Universe for ever and God shall be all in all. Think what that story will be when we get to know it!

Who is to continue that Life of Christ for us? Are the angels writing it now in the Libraries of Heaven? Shall our great writers on earth go on with it when they get there? Shall you and I read it one day when we go to that Land "when the books are opened in Heaven"?

I feel quite excited as I think of what is before us!

Fancy our reading some day that Life of Christ! I was going to write "THE END" at the close of this book. But my pen refuses to write it now. For this is not the end. The grandest part remains still to be told us. I can only wonderingly put down at the close of my little story:

"TO BE CONTINUED."

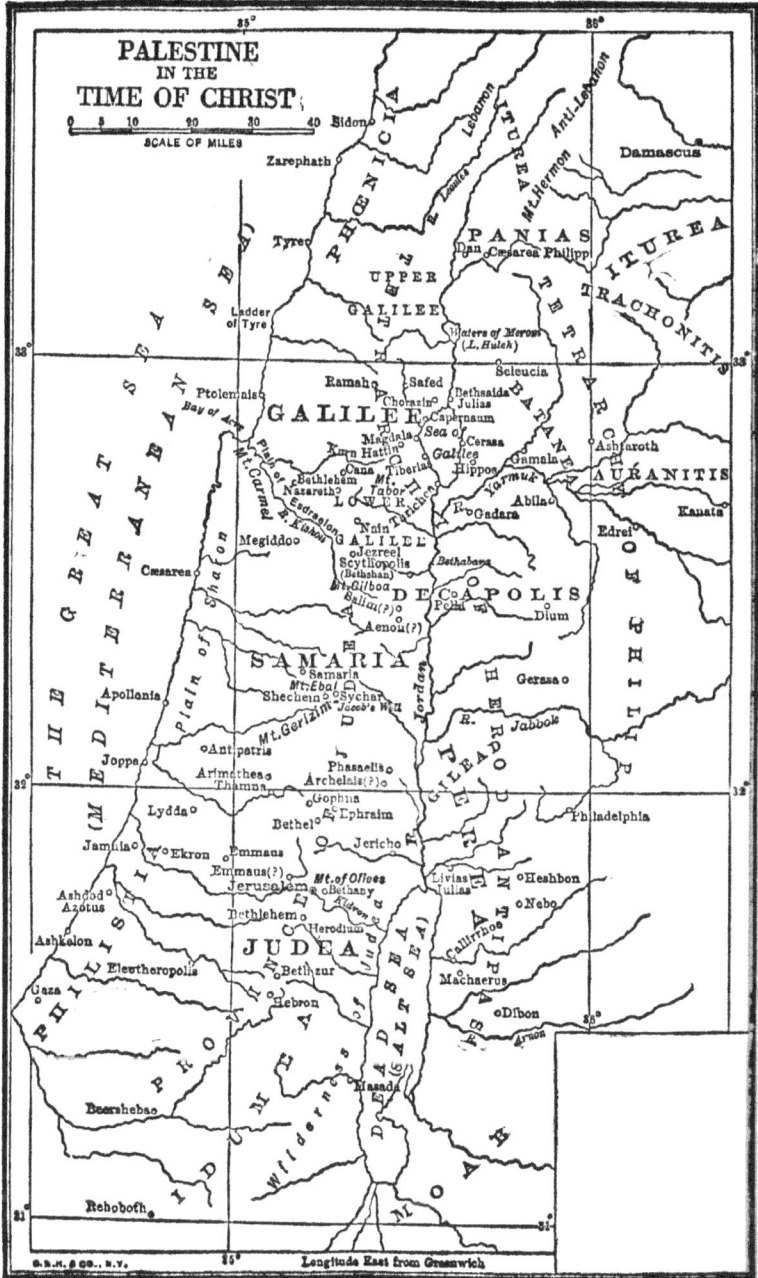

PALESTINE
IN THE
TIME OF CHRIST

SCALE OF MILES
0   5   10   20   30   40

Longitude East from Greenwich

www.ingramcontent.com/pod-product-compliance
Lightning Source LLC
Chambersburg PA
CBHW021048090426
42738CB00006B/242